Dear Libra
Caitlin
Thank you for Sharing
your Joy & Love.

EVERYTHING IS
A CHOICE

Live a Life
Worth Living ♡

Brittany E.

EVERYTHING IS A CHOICE

THROUGH A COACH'S EYES

BRITTANY EHRICK

JONES MEDIA
PUBLISHING

Jones Media Publishing
10645 N. Tatum Blvd. Ste. 200-166
Phoenix, AZ 85028
www.JonesMediaPublishing.com

Printed in the United States of America

ISBN-13: 978-1-945849-65-7 paperback

CONTENTS

ACKNOWLEDGMENTS

When I started writing my book, I thought that this process was a one-man-show. I now know that it takes a village of dedicated people to write a book to help people change, grow, take action, and be their very best. I didn't know how large a village it would take to create my own version of a masterpiece of growth and healthling. I didn't count along the way, but I know there were tons of people who helped me create my book. Thank you to everyone who supported me and helped me throughout this process.

TAYLOR

Thank you to the best husband in the whole world. Thank you for constantly reading and editing my book. I know that I lived and breathed the book and coaching and, in turn, so did you. Thank you for supporting me through my unhealthy thoughts and fears. Also, thank you for the financial sacrifices you made because of my learning disabilities. I will be forever grateful for your support in helping me be the inspirational author and Life Coach I am today. Thank you for being selfless in this process and for all your dedication. Thank you for helping me become successful in our life together. I love you forever and ever.

ROSS AND ROSIE

Thank you so much to the best parents that I could have asked for. Both of you put so much time and effort and care into my book. You both cared so much about my success and happiness, which was everything I needed to step forward in my vulnerability. I love how you surprised me in loving the cover of the book. I appreciate all the creativity you saw in my cover and book, as well as the creativity you brought to my book. I most definitely needed the support you gave me with my book and throughout my life. You both mean the world to me and I am beyond lucky to call you my family. I love you both more than you will ever know. Thank you for all the effort and hard work you put into the gift I have created for my readers. I know they will appreciate you, too.

AUNT ROXY, GRANDMA JANE, AND GREAT-GRANDMA EVELYN

Thank goodness my Aunt Roxy, Grandma Jane, and Great-Grandma Evelyn provided me some good memories to look back on, as I have very few fond memories of my childhood. I am grateful for all the love they showed me.

I want to thank my aunt for giving me everything you could give me at that time: the love and support, along with the home you gave me, for as long as you could. You made all the difference for me. You stepped up when no one else would. You showed up for me when I needed you. You cared when nobody else would. You fed me when nobody else would feed me. You were what I needed during that really hard time in my life. Thank you very much for your sacrifices.

I must thank my Grandma Jane and her mother, Evelyn. Great-Grandma Evelyn was incredible at listening and making great memories with me. We would drink hot tea with milk (which I still do today), we would talk, and we created games together. She was always there when I needed someone to listen to what I had to say; Grandma Evelyn was great at listening without judgment and with empathy. Her daughter, Grandma Jane, is someone I will forever be grateful for as well, for many reasons. One reason being that I wasn't her blood—she was my stepdad's mom, and yet she still loved me. She gave me the gift of love and happiness. We baked and cooked together. I have so many great memories of us and the cafeteria.

JOHN AND ABBY

People of all denominations took me in throughout my childhood. I want to thank all the strangers who cared for me. I'm eternally grateful to the foster organization called CASA (Court Appointed Special Adovate). My CASA foster grandparents, Abby and John, were great gifts to me. They went above and beyond to make sure I had the love and support I so desperately needed. They also did whatever they could to help me have fun, and they taught me to express my emotions in cool, creative ways. For example, John is an artist and helped me learn to paint my feelings out. Above all else, they taught me the true love of God. These people loved me and treated me the way that all kids wish to be loved by their grandparents.

Thank you so much for all the time and love that you gave me even though you didn't have to. I am so grateful for you, to this day. Thank you, Abby and John.

NICOLE JAMES, CATHY, ALLI, AND CAMBRIA

I want to thank my editors and typists, who sat on the other side of computer screens for endless hours. You guys helped me in making my words come to life. Without you I don't know how I would put my words on paper. I want to thank you guys for sitting with me while I wrote the most vulnerable parts of my book and for holding the space for me to cry, write out my story, and bare my soul. Some of you wept with me, and some of you simply held the space that I needed. You made my writing experience so much more beautiful because you were on the journey of writing with me.

I want to thank my helper Nicole James for taking my raw recordings and putting them on paper. Also, thank you for listening to hours and hours of me creating my book and deciphering my thoughts. It was really incredible to speak to you and your daughter directly when I was writing. Thank you for that space.

Now I want to thank Cathy, who took the written recordings and turned them into paragraphs with me. I want to thank you for dealing with the beautiful messiness of being my helper. I am grateful for the time you put in and the bonding it created. Thank you for creating good memories with me as a friend and as a helper in my book. Without your help, being the middleman, I don't know where I would be. Thank you for your hours, dedication, tears, love, and pure selflessness.

Thank you, Alli, for the time, space, and energy that you put into this book. It was incredible to work with someone who is creative and outside of the box like me. I want to thank you for the love and the bonding we created during this process. Thank you for sharing your deep story with me and my readers; it changed me. More than anything, thank you for letting me coach you through it. It was an honor to coach you and to call you my friend.

As you can see, there were a lot of stages to my book, but I was always looking for a person who could help me type, spell, and read. More importantly, someone who could keep up with me and elevate me to the next level of writing. I didn't realize that this person would be seventeen years old, in high school and college at the same time, and would be someone I could create a bond with that would last a lifetime. This girl's name is Cambria Espree Hatch. Thank you so much for your love, commitment, and support.

COACHES

To become an author, I needed a mini-network of coaches and hypnotherapists in my life and in my book to ensure that I was not misunderstood due to my learning disabilities. The people who helped me in this book as coaches and as educators are Kerri Myers, Larnette Winston, Sherry Gilbert, Gianina Monroe, and Amy Everhart. These amazing ladies gave me some insight when they were coaching or hypnotizing me. I am forever grateful for all that they have done. Most of all, I am thankful that they helped me allow readers to understand me clearly.

I am so appreciative of Larnette for her passion in helping me share my wisdom with others and for her help in repeatedly editing my book from beginning to end; ensuring that my voice was never misunderstood throughout the book and in my practice. With her detail-oriented approach, Larnette was definitely the finisher I was looking and praying for. Thank you for the coaching you provided me around my book and for helping me to confidently stand in my power of being an author. I want to thank you for your sisterhood. I am so honored that you shared your story and journey with me and my readers. I am proud to be your Life Coach, but I am most proud of our friendship, the space we can hold for each other, and gifts that we, as coaches, share with the world.

Kerri Myers is amazing. She has coached me through my fears and doubts about the book and so much more. She helped me become the inspirational coach and author that I am today. I want to thank Kerri for the numerous hours she vested in me as an individual and my growth. Thank you, Kerri, for your support.

Thank you, girls, for always believing in me. I am just so lucky to have these people who care about me and want to see others be free through the techniques in my book. I know I can do anything and everything with a team like this behind me.

Thank you to all the other coaches who supported me along the way who are not specifically named.

NATHAN AND AMANDA TANQUARY, ALISA GRIGSBY, AND AMANDA HALE

I want to show my appreciation for Nathan and Amanda Tanquary and Alisa Grigsby for spending thirty-one days with me in the ICU and for always helping me through the ups and downs of my medical condition. I want to thank Nathan, Amanda T., Alisa, and Amanda H. for being my family throughout all my health endeavors. They are so understanding, they always have my back, and they never judge me. Also, I am grateful for the friendship that my health has created between us. I want to thank you guys for being so certain and confident about my book and my company.

DEB AND RANDY

I want to thank Deb and Randy from the bottom of my heart for taking me into your home as though I were your own, especially during my medical journey. You helped with the loneliness of my husband being gone and so much more. You gave me understanding of what a beautiful and romantic marriage is and how safe it can be. You also taught me what it was like to be a real leader and how to lead with my heart. I had the motivation to strive to be a leader because of the things you taught me. Finally, I want to thank you for the incredible friendship you gave me and familyhood.

MY CLIENTS

Thank you to all my clients who were vulnerable enough to share your stories and allow those stories to be in my book to help others. Also, thank you to the people in my family who allowed their stories to be shared as well. Thank you to all my clients who trusted me enough to allow me to coach them and to the clients who have practiced the techniques in my book.

FAMILY MEMBERS

Thank you to all the Poarras' for the support, love, and encouragement. Thank you to mom for teaching me the rawness of life and for loving me as much as you could. Thank you to my stepfather for loving me without limits when you didn't have to and for teaching me to have fun.

AN ALL-AROUND THANKYOU

To everybody who helped me that I cannot name, I want to thank you from the bottom of my heart for your efforts. Thank you to the people who listened to me over the phone and typed/spelled for me; I am very grateful for your contribution. I also want to thank all the silent friends and family members who listened to me endlessly talk about my book. Most importantly, I want to thank everyone who reads my book and gains clarity from the things I have shared. I hope you learn something new. Thank you for your precious time.

INTRODUCTION

Do you want to learn how to find confidence, trust, faith and life's true beauty? How about solutions for overcoming the things in life that may be holding you back, such as people-pleasing, limited beliefs, button-pushing, and stress? Do you ever notice your unhealthy thought patterns and cycles that get in the way of achieving your true desires? Do you want to learn how to be present and not react to situations? Do you want the gift of finding your true self? Do you want to be able to turn your pain into good, so you can make a difference in the world? Do you want to achieve freedom from everything that is holding you back from being the best you?

If you answered yes to any or all these questions, hold on tight because you are about to board the roller coaster ride of your life. On this roller coaster ride, I hope you can lose yourself in the heaviness and beauty of what life is all about.

During this exciting and liberating journey, I encourage you to allow my book to be your trusted partner. *Everything Is a Choice* can help you through your pain and suffering. This journey can help you face the hard truths of your reality and give you the necessary tools to work through it. This book can motivate you to change and to be the person you wish to be. I've created an opportunity for you to see me as your own personal Life Coach, guiding you through the words I've written. I know that some may be unable to invest in Life Coaching or may not have the have the time to commit to the coaching process. This is why I did everything I could to share my full life, my skills, and my resources with you through these pages.

Imagine that my voice is always with you. The techniques and inspiration that follow are meant to guide you and give you the fuel and confidence you need to move on to the next stages of your journey. My hope is that through my own story and the stories of my clients, you will see that you have partners who have gone through this transformation, too.

I wholeheartedly believe that this book and my story can change your life; I hope it does. I have turned my entire life upside down to become the Life Coach I am today—for God, for my own personal growth, for my marriage, for my client's' success, and now, for you. I became a Life Coach for the sake of individuals who are looking for a new direction with more choices. I also became a coach for the people who are ready for change and growth, the people who don't know how to find it and feared it.

When you are going through your own pain and suffering, you are just so blinded by it. You don't feel like there are any options for you to get out. When you are in the hurt, you can't recognize why it is there; you can't see what good could possibly come from it. In the moment, all you know is that you want to do everything you can to shield yourself from the pain and hurt. You are blind to the good that will come out of such moments and what you will learn from the pain in the long run. *Everything Is a Choice* is meant to show you that good can come out of the hardships of life; sometimes you just have to work for it.

This book will take you on an adventure you will never forget! It is very personal, detailed, encouraging, and emotionally engaging. In my opinion, my book is both draining and uplifting, like everything in life.

I want to thank you for taking the time to read *Everything Is a Choice*; it means the world to me. Dive in, enjoy, and stay with it. Don't give up! While you're reading, I hope you allow yourself to learn what you want to learn about yourself and see how much you will change and grow. The possibilities of self-discovery are endless if you open yourself up in safe spaces and allow yourself to be vulnerable to who you are and what you need to change. Who knows what you will uncover and receive with the new information? Please keep an open mind while working through this book. I wrote about my own vulnerabilities so that you can have the opportunity to be vulnerable for yourself.

Please note that this book is based on my perspective, my experiences, and where I came from. I can only share with you the stories and experiences that I went through personally. To protect myself and others, I have to be careful what I share about my past and my clients as well as how much detail I provide, but I am grateful that I can share with you what I think is appropriate and right. One of the biggest reasons I wrote my book this way is because I want it to be read by all ages; some details simply aren't appropriate.

I hope you can be open to my unique way of educating and awakening readers to new opportunities and growth. I am teaching from my life experiences and through the professional education I have received, as well as where I stand now in my life.

I will push you—that is a guarantee! However, if you lean in without resisting, I think you'll realize that you are capable of doing the impossible: changing your life. The rewards of having a healthy life are endless. If I can do it and my clients can do it, then so can you!

1

WHAT MADE ME WHO I AM

TRIBULATIONS

When you are a child you always fantasize that your parents met in the most beautiful and romantic way possible, with intentions of starting their dream family. A family where you eat every meal together and pray over it before you eat. Where you go to church together every Sunday and every holiday. Where you take goofy matching-sweater photos to send out at the holidays. Where you make family traditions that continue for generations and brings warmth and comfort that last a lifetime. Your family is what every family strives to be. It's a family where you get together for every momentous occasion, including Packer games. Where you just get together for the fun of it because you love each other and miss each other. Where you show up for each other no matter what, whether it's big or small, especially in times of need. Where you have two parents at events like games and recitals. The typical white picket fence family home where you go get ice cream after a hard day's chores that, of course, you all do together, as a family. This is the family I married into, my husband's family, the Ehricks.

Well, that's not how I grew up, not in the slightest.

To start, I need to make something very clear, there is extreme significance to the terms "Dad" and "Mom." These titles, these terms of endearment, are earned by being the parent—the parent who takes care of you, shows up for you, protects you, and loves you. I've never felt like my biological or adopted parents deserved or desired to be my mom and dad. Your parents should always try to set aside their problems to teach you to be the best you by setting the best example. Your parents should be emotionally and mentally mature enough to stop acting out and stop the behaviors they are telling you not to engage in. A parent is someone who freely gives unconditional love and acceptance and who leads you to be the leader of your life and guides you to make the best decisions for *yourself*.

That being said, the parents who earned the titles of Mom and Dad in my life are my husband, Taylor's incredible parents, who treated me the best out of all of the parent figures who were around me throughout my life. Taylor's parents have shown me so much unconditional love and affection that I cannot begin to compare them to any other parent figures I've had in my life. You can't get any better than the Ehricks. Ross and Rose became my mama and papa bear. For the first time in my life, I was treated as someone's very own! I am proud to be an Ehrick

WHAT MADE ME WHO I AM

after having been so many other names in the past; I never felt like any of those names were mine. I felt like an outcast and a weirdo at times because I never felt like I belonged to those other families. That's one of the reasons I use epithets such as *biological, genetic, birth, hereditary,* and *blood-related* mother and father when I refer to my birth family. As well as to help clarify my family tree.

HOW I WAS BROUGHT INTO THE WORLD

It all began with my biological mother, Emily, and biological father, Cody, and how they met. Emily and Cody met in a bar. Their short-lived relationship was a stream of fun and partying. Essentially, they were friends with benefits; I was the consequence. (Wow! How those words made me feel unwanted, sad, and overall, just not good enough.) I felt totally and completely abandoned, but that wasn't the first time I had been abandoned and abused; no, the first time I ever felt this way was when I was in the womb, not even born yet, because my birth father could not control his rage. Over the course of the next several years, all of those awful feelings escalated and intensified.

WHAT MY BIOLOGICAL FATHER BROUGHT TO MY LIFE

When my birth father found out Emily was pregnant with me, he lashed out and physically abused her while she was still pregnant with me. He strangled her to the point where she could not speak for a whole week. After beating her (and me), he left forever, tragically leaving my poor mom behind, scared and alone causing more insecurities for both of us. I have never met my birth father, which I have always struggled with, and it led me to wonder: Why did he leave me? Was I not worthy of his love and affection?

When I was just about thirteen, I was told that my biological father was a pedophile who was incarcerated for sexually abusing his stepdaughter. As if being abandoned weren't enough for little me to deal with, now I was the daughter of a pedophile. Basically, my identity at just thirteen years old was an accidental, unwanted daughter of a drug addict and an abusive pedophile. When I was young, I was left questioning what did my future hold? If I was from *them*, what did that make me? I thought that it meant that I couldn't do good in the world because I came from such evil. The questions about abandonment and not feeling like I was good enough have always lingered in my mind. These questions became more apparent because, throughout my childhood, I was shoved around to friends, foster homes, respite homes, kinship homes, adoptive homes, relatives, and random strangers. Until the Ehricks took me in, I had lived with more than a dozen families and friends of my biological mother. I was constantly exposed to some of the most horrific and violent scenarios imaginable; these were situations no one should ever have to experience, let alone a child. The questions about myself and my biological family grew as more and more bad occurred.

However, I would be open someday to hearing my biological father's side of the story and share that I have forever forgiven him.

MY ONE SHOT AT A NORMAL FAMILY

My mother met my dream dad and her perfect husband when I was six weeks old. They were the perfect fit because they could bond over their shared past with drugs and alcohol and they had me to bond over, too. My stepfather did stop hard drugs before he met my biological mother, but he and Emily still got high off of marijuana together while they were married.

I thought we were finally happy. My stepfather and mom got married when I was about nine months old. I'm sure it felt amazing to have a dad like him. When I was little, I always believed he was more than worthy of the title "Dad." He brought joy and safety to my life.

Quickly after getting married, my biological mother and stepfather had a son together, my little (half) brother. I finally had the potential for a true family. Wow! I was excited to have a baby brother, a friend to play with, and a brother to grow up. We were going to protect each other, stand up for each other, have each other's back, tell each other our secrets, pull pranks together, and raise our future children together so they would have cute cousins to play and bond with. We were going to have it all. The simplicity of having a mom and dad around was our dream life. At that time, this was our reality.

However, our perfect dream family did not last long. During their marriage, my biological mother began to experiment with drugs, again. She was always high on something or drinking or both. In fact, she was running a drug lab with her friends/boyfriends in the back of the many different white trash travel trailers we lived in. I remember feeling so scared and unsure why I was a part of her latent lifestyle. This part of my childhood took me a long time to let go of because I felt like she didn't care about me and I wasn't important enough for her to change. It was painful, feeling like I was not worthy of being loved and protected from the harm she was inflicting on both of us. I always wished she would have shown up for me and taken care of me like she was supposed to. I longed for her to be the type of mom that was there for me, to talk to, to help me learn, and to teach me how to become a woman. I just wanted her to be the mom, but at the time, she simply couldn't. She self-sabotaged and had a tendency to cause problems for herself, me, and everyone around her.

The final blow to my stepdad's and mother's marriage occurred when Emily was about thirty years old. My stepdad caught her cheating on him with a nineteen-year-old boy; this and the drug labs resulted in a violent divorce. What I saw happen the night that my stepfather found out about my biological mother's cheating still haunts me to this day. I will never unhear the screeching of my own screams.

THE DEVASTATING DIVORCE

Here's how I was dragged through the devastatingly violent mess that many call divorce.

In his own way, my stepfather made great strides to obtain custody of my younger brother and me, but even with all of his efforts, he was only granted custody of my brother because I was not his biological daughter. This broke me because I was left to take care of myself at age seven without any help or know-how. My biological mother would just leave me with her sister to clean up her mess.

My first of many memories of violence took place when my stepfather came to claim custody of my baby brother from my mother. We all met at a park and I remember sitting and playing in the dirt, as children often do, completely oblivious to the impending violence that was about to occur. When my stepfather arrived, my mother, as usual, was strung out on drugs and verbally and physically attacked him with unbridled hatred. She'd brought her boyfriend and some of her tweaker friends for backup in case things got violently heated (which they always did). My blood mother was very vindictive when she was threatened and high, and she apparently had intentions of sabotaging the relinquishing of my brother because what mother would voluntarily give up her child? How painful this must have been for her.

The next thing I remember was being shocked and terrified because my mother's boyfriend was abruptly taken down to the ground with extreme force by my stepdad's dad (who served in a branch of the military), followed by the barrel of a gun shoved into his forehead, which imprinted the shape of the barrel into his skin. I also remember seeing the barrel of a gun in Emily's mouth. I was terrified for her life and I was thinking, "Why would someone do that?" I felt so scared as I sat there all by myself, watching the horrific scene unfold right in front of me. I wonder how my brother must have felt being the rope in a game of tug-a-war between my birth mother and stepfather. I thought, why is this happening to our family? Why do bad things keep happening to me? Hadn't I been through enough?

I watched everything I knew and loved leave without me. I felt so alone and deprived as I watched my stepfather drive away with my brother and realized that any chance of a good or even normal childhood was leaving with them.

That was the last time I saw my baby brother for quite some time. This was very hard for me. to be taken away from my brother because I really loved him and wanted to be with him and my stepfather. I, being so young, I didn't understand why we were apart. After all the awfulness that had transpired, there I was, left to go home with my strung-out mother and her abusive boyfriend, not knowing what further violence would occur.

CELEBRATING MY BROTHER'S BIRTHDAY

I am unsure how much time passed, perhaps about six months to a year. However long it had been, I was finally able to see my younger brother for his birthday. I was elated because I had missed him so much. It was fun to eat cake and ice cream together and just get to be kids for once. I remember having a great time playing with him, and all seemed fine until we had to leave. We had to go back to the trailer per my birth mother's psycho boyfriend's demand that we come home immediately. He, the bad man, was crazy, controlling, extremely jealous, and insecure.

My stepfather reluctantly offered to drive my birth mother and me home since, as per usual, she had been using. My stepfather put himself in a bad situation to protect me from my high mother and her awful boyfriend.

When we pulled up to our trailer, the bad man came out with a look of intense hatred in his eyes, as though he were ready to kill. At that point, he and my mother instigated yet another event I never wanted to be a part of and that I will never forget. Things quickly became heated as my stepfather's girlfriend, who had been drinking, got out of the car and started telling my mother's boyfriend to calm down. However, the bad man wasn't going to let anyone talk to him in any way he didn't like. He punched my stepfather's girlfriend in the face, knocking her to the ground. He didn't care about the sacred law not to touch women. Let's just say he had no respect or boundaries because, frankly, he was an animal. The horrid fight began with ax handles and bats as I watched from the front seat of the car, terrified that everybody I loved would be killed by the bad man. Finally, after so much destruction to my life and family, my stepfather decided to be the bigger person. He chose to turn around, stop fighting and left; once again leaving me behind.

Later, I found out that after this horrible event went down, my brave, courageous stepfather turned himself in to the police. (Thankfully, the charges would be dropped.) And oh, how I wished he had taken me with him when he left because the events of the night did not end there.

GUEST-STARRING THE BAD MAN

Later that dreadful evening, my mom was beaten to a pulp by her horrendous boyfriend with the handle of the bad man's gun; again, this was right in front of me. All I could do was stand there, frozen in shock and disbelief, as more blood was spilled. Not only was my neighborhood destroyed by the vehicle that took out anything in its way, but many people were severely injured. I remember wishing, hoping it was all just a bad dream, praying that there wasn't any more hurt to take out on me.

Sadly, all the violence of that night still wasn't enough for him. The bad man hurt the only friends I had, my little baby orange kittens. These little kitties were my best friends, my one way to receive love; they made me feel safe and not all alone. One by one, he threw them against the wall, instantly killing them, as I watched with tear-filled eyes.

And apparently, that still wasn't enough destruction for him in his high-out-of-his-mind state. The bad man shattered an entire fish tank on me with all the water and fish still in it. There were shards of glass in my hair and all over my body, and I was drenched. I wished for God to save me and my baby kittens right then and there.

Any leftover of anger or physical aggression was taken out on me, as always. My mother and I left in an ambulance, with more than just physical wounds to heal.

TOSSED AROUND FROM PERSON TO PERSON

The first time Child Protective Services (CPS) came into my life was when I was nine months old. And again, CPS came to take me to live with my aunt, my biological mom's older sister. This was normal because every time something went wrong, I was shipped off to my aunt's, and every time Emily seemed to be doing okay, I was sent back to her. So, unfortunately, this change in households was only temporary. They consistently sent me back to live with my mother because they wrongfully thought she was doing better with her problems (drugs). And I probably ended up begging to be with my biological mom because what child doesn't want her mom? Of course, it didn't occur to me then that my family should have done something, anything to get me out of that insane situation. Now I wish they would have at least tried to save me from my mother. I wish they would have placed me in a real foster home as a young girl, so I could have avoided the extremely dangerous situations that caused me severe emotional and physical pain.

MY AUNT'S SACRIFICES

I was always really close to my biological mom's older sister, my aunt; this is what she will be referred to as in the book. She became my "kinship"/foster parent, but neither of us ever referred to her that way. I just called her my aunt. Although I became close to her, my time with her and her family did not last long enough. My aunt housed me on and off from the time I was four years old till I was about eleven. My aunt gave me everything she could, and without her, I would be nothing. My aunt tried to do what she could, which makes me grateful for the time I was with her, which unfortunately did not last long enough.

WISHING FOR PERMANENCE

The frequent abandonment that transpired during my childhood was crushing. I was always being sent or taken to a new place of residence. I stayed at these new places for different lengths of time: sometimes days, sometimes weeks, and sometimes months. There were a few families and relatives I stayed with for longer periods of time, but whenever a crisis occurred in those families—and they occurred often—guess who was again sent to live with someone else? A young innocent child who did not belong to anyone! I, again, had no place to go and no family to speak of, unless I went to stay with my aunt. At times, I was with my biological mother at her latest temporary living space, and other times (most times), she was just gone, having left no hint to where she was, where she was going, or if she was okay (which she wasn't). I always felt as if this sporadic movement didn't matter to her, especially because she was so out of it that she was clueless to all the pain that she put me through.

Moving was about the only constant in my life—well, besides chaos and havoc. Although I'm sure I was a challenge at times (because I was extremely emotional, as anyone would expect), I don't think I was a bad kid. I rarely acted out or got into trouble like most children do. However, I did have massive outbursts due to the pain and loss that I went through. As a matter a fact, as an adult, I was told that I had been a sweet, kind girl who was terrified of the world.

Since the families I lived with were often very poor and had their own problems, I was the low man on the totem pole when anything went wrong. To them, I was just a favor to my biological mother. I can remember thinking, *what is wrong with me? Why doesn't anybody want to keep me and call me their own?*

WHAT FEARS I HAD TO OVERCOME

The abuse continued throughout my childhood. Unfortunately, the physical beatings I received were not the most painful thing I suffered through. Although I have tried to forget, the worst of my memories are still crystal clear in my mind. They include the pain of cigarettes being put out on my body by my biological mother's strung-out friends and the physical and mental scars that it left. I will spare you the details of the other scars I have from these people, however, this made me feel isolated and caused me to not trust adults.

Until I was about twenty-five years of age, I was exceedingly skittish, jumpy, and fearful when adults moved too fast around me. I was always overly aware of every possible exit and my surroundings, everywhere I went. This was mainly because when I was little, I was shown that adults (the people I am supposed to look up to) could do anything to me and my body. When I was young, my biological mother and her many different sexual partners would forget or ignore that I was there. These terrible adults would drip steaming hot candle wax onto me while they were having sex *right above me* or when I was in the same bed with them in our little white trash travel trailer. The pain was unbearable, but I couldn't say a word out of fear of retributions.

The saddest part for me was that I knew this situation wasn't normal or right, but I had no way out. Sometimes I would be brave and courageous enough to try to save my mother and myself by telling the school nurse about the horrific things occurring in my life, but it only made matters worse, as my biological mom's peeps and her terrible boyfriends would just beat me more. I was always blamed for our multitude of problems. In fact, my mother and her boyfriends would try to keep me from going to school (the only place I ever felt truly safe). They even had the audacity to come to the school and try to kidnap me even though my biological mother wasn't legally allowed to see me because she and her boyfriends were too dangerous to be around. Imagine how it felt to have your mother try to steal you from school. Imagine what other kids must have been thinking about me and how hard it was for me to get any schoolwork done.

One of the most disappointing things about my childhood was that my mother never thought any of these dreadful events were abnormal. I didn't like my life and the chaos that surrounded me, but where was I to go? I was so scared, and I had no one to stand up for me, and I did not know how to stand up for myself. What was I to do? She was my mother. She was all I had.

MY DEEP-ROOTED FEAR

The sexual and the physical abuse was a whole other ball game of deep-rooted fears. As a result, I had a fear of men until I was twenty-five years old. It took a very long time for me to be able to trust any man. I'm not sure if it was the physical or sexual abuse that I was more afraid of, but either way, it was a long, hard road to endure and even more difficult to overcome.

These extreme fears came from strangers, my biological mother's friends, and her multiple boyfriends, who would take advantage of me, physically hurt me, and/or molest me. I had an extreme phobia of men. This trepidation about men manifested frequently into panic attacks and full-blown flashbacks, as though it were happening all over again. I would freak out or freeze whenever I was alone with a man, fearing they would hurt me and do unspeakable things to me. My stay-away feelings and actions towards men only heightened as more and more men did wrong to me. Of course, this caused me to have a severe lack of trust when it came to men. I always felt as if all men were angry, violent, and womanizers. I didn't want to let men in because I'd been shown time and time again that they were self-centered and cruel and didn't deserve trust or love. No man in my life had ever been there for me, so why trust men? What was the point?

This section of the book is dedicated to all the men who helped me trust again. I want to thank them from the bottom of my heart for building my trust. Without these men, I would still believe that there are no good men in the world, that all men are going to take advantage of me. So, thank you to all the adopted uncles, nanny jobs, and, of course, the biggest game changer of all: my husband, Taylor, and his dad, "Papa Bear." These men helped me correct my fear of unwanted touching of my body from men. Without these amazing men in my life, I would still be petrified and burdened by the fear that the worst that men could do to me or would want to do to me would happen to me. Later, I met the good men that I still have in my life and everything changed, even though it took a long time.

At this point in my life, I absolutely love coaching men and working with them in a professional setting. Thanks to one of my first male clients, James, and one of my lawyer clients.

From the bottom of my heart, thank you all for healing me and helping me let go. Building the broken trust one man at a time, was the way I was able to heal from my fears and insecurities with men. It took bravery, courage, and trust from both parties to triumph over my phobia. For the process to start, it took trusting Taylor. If you struggle with trusting abuse, see if starting by trusting one person helps you. There are good and trustworthy men that are there to help you, too. When you're in this process, make sure that—that man is worthy and a safe choice.

How School Was a Constant Struggle

As you can probably guess by now, my education was not a priority in my biological mother's eyes, because she didn't have the ability to prioritize. She also couldn't read or write. Fortunately, when I was at my aunt's house, she did her best to tutor me even though she had other children to take care of. I'm sure it didn't help my aunt's cause when I had my emotional outburst due to my lack of understanding.

When I first started school, it was an instant struggle. I was in some incredible special ed classes, the kind where there are swings hanging from the ceiling and thick blue mats on the floor and the walls to protect the children. This learning environment was perfect for me as a child. I remember playing with beads and learning how to pick them up. I remember learning how to hold a pencil. But I also remember how much I struggled and how hard I had to work to just learn how to write the alphabet, let alone my own name. This was also the room where I did tons of speech therapy and learned how to talk. I was probably in this creative space until I was about ten years old. Thank you to all the teachers who worked to teach me all those many years.

In kindergarten, my aunt was told that I would never be able to read because I saw words backward and upside down. I just couldn't process a word as a word. The concept didn't exist in my head, and they told her it might never exist. They also told her that they didn't think I would ever be able to function enough to read or write. (We now know that they were incorrect, because with hard work and dedication, I overcame that challenge. I mean, look at me now—I wrote this book.)

Throughout elementary school, I rarely spent time in a normal classroom; I spent my time in a class for students with learning disabilities, all the way through to sixth grade. After those years of playing catch-up, though, I finally got the opportunity to get into a mainstream classroom as a seventh grader. During my schooling years, I was mocked when I read or even spoke aloud. This gave me the identity of being ignorant and a waste of space that needed to live in silence.

Being viewed as stupid was yet another challenge for me. The teasing and feelings of inadequacy were so hurtful. People called me names like "stupid" and "slow"; the names that caused me to call myself were far worse than what anybody else could have said to me. Despite that, I kept pushing through as always, just trying to fit in and be normal. I wanted to be up-to-speed like everybody else and not be left behind. I wanted to not be confused, and I wanted to be able to read and write because I knew it was so important to making it in this world. It was so frustrating not being able to do something that was supposed to come easy. I thought there wouldn't be a spot for me in the world—that the world would abandon me—if I didn't have these skills.

Now I write, read, and spell at a second- to fourth-grade level. To be completely honest, I am proud of the progress I have made in my literacy skills. I can't help but be impressed with the fact that I have written an entire book!

I would like to say I am so grateful for my disabilities. They allow me to see the world in a unique light, and I have met so many amazing people because of them. I wouldn't change my story for the world.

HOW EMILY'S ADDICTIONS STOLE OUR LIFE

My biological mother was an obsessive, abusive, and needy woman. I remember almost always being concerned for my safety while living with her, constantly fearing the future, especially since her lifestyle was extremely unpredictable, unhealthy, and overall extremely out of control. Looking back, I realize she needed me to take care of her. I had to become the adult, trying to take care of both of us. I thought it was so unfair that it became my job to take care of her and hold her when she was hurting even though I never got that love and comfort in return. It is a mother's job to take care of her child, not a daughter's job to take care of her mother.

I feel like I missed out on my entire childhood because of the many emotional problems she passed on to me. I had to grow up super-fast for her sake and for the sake of my own survival. As a young child, I had a difficult time explaining my living arrangements, and my situation biological mother's drug problem to the people in my life. I would frequently drop my massive emotional bombs of truth on people. These bombs were me telling people the pure truth of the abuse my biological mother caused by turning a blind eye to what was going on.

Drugs and alcohol were a constant struggle for my biological mother. I can count on one hand the few times, growing up that I saw her sober. Her lies, her self-doubt, her unconscious manipulation, her destructive personality, and her insecurities about love were a constant reminder of the chaos of what my life had become.

Now, as a coach, I can see that she was lost and used drugs to cope and self-medicate. I have to say I have no regrets about the way I was raised because without her as my biological mother, I could not be me and I would not be able to help as many people as I have. I love who I am and what I bring to the world.

PRISON

Throughout my childhood and into my early adult years, my mother spent time in and out of prison. I remember how devastating, terrifying, and degrading it felt, even as a young adult, to visit my mother in prison. The experience taught me that I did not want to be anything like her. I could not imagine being so bad that you have to be gruesomely searched before visiting with your daughter. She literally had to be stripped for an extremely invasive body search for any contraband she may have been in possession of. She was searched like this from head to toe for many years of her life. How that must have made her feel ashamed and inhuman. After the interrogation of her whole body, she had to come see me and be happy. I felt so sorry for her. It was unquestionably hard for me to watch her struggle with the bad choices she made in her life and the consequences of her actions.

She feared the world and taught me to be the same and to always expect the worst. She lacked the faith and the hope that there was any good in the world. It was a powerful life lesson to watch her blow her whole life away because of her vast emotional pain. Don't get me wrong—the suffering my birth mother went through was awfully messed up. However, her consciously and unconsciously choosing to repeat these screwed up patterns, made everything worse for herself and me. She just let the bad things that happened to her happen to me as well. When it came to me, though, these patterns escalated dramatically, so I made the choice at a young age that I was going to stop this craziness and not be like her or allow her patterns to repeat.

Ironically, we bonded while she was in prison. We talked about the painful things she put me through. She wasn't always ready to own up to what she did, but she was there listening to my pain and helping heal my soul as well as my damaged inner child. I consider the time we spent together while she was sober in prison to be good times because that's when she was closest to be the mom I always longed for and needed. It took me a long while to get through all the fear, pain, and guilt of leaving her every week after creating our bonding moments. It felt like I was never going to see her again.

My mother did some cool things for me while she was in prison that supported my healing. One thing I loved was when she sent me handwritten letters. I thought this was awesome because we both have severe dyslexia and can't read or spell.

Our letters were pretty funny. It was like we had our own language because neither of us could write for the life of us. We wrote each other almost every week. We wrote about everything going on in our lives, like Taylor and I getting married and past events that had gotten in our way throughout life. I wrote about my full-ride volleyball scholarship, and she designed handmade artwork for me. She also wrote and drew me beautiful, sweet, tear-jerking cards that I still have and cherish today. The cards gave me happiness. Finally, my mother loved me, in her own way. I will always be grateful that God put my mother in prison, because her incarceration protected her and gave me the wonderful opportunity to get to know a mother who loved me very much.

WHAT IT'S LIKE TO HAVE A HOMELESS PARENT

My biological mother may still be alive and on the streets, selling herself and begging for money, as she was the last time I saw her. I don't know her current situation, but I think about her and pray for her always.

The last time I saw her was when I was hospitalized at age twenty. She came to visit me, and it was clear that she was losing her sobriety, lying to me and herself again, and toxic to my well-being. I'll be honest: although I do not pursue any connection with her, I am still curious to know if she is still alive and okay. Sometimes my family and I get calls about her being stabbed or asking about her whereabouts because she witnessed a murder and a severe beating. No matter what, she is still my mom and I love her and care about her in ways I cannot explain. If she is happy with this lifestyle, then I am happy for her. I do not judge her for her actions, or lack thereof, because it is her life to live. But with her unhealthy choices, she cannot be in my life. This does not mean that I don't grieve and miss her sometimes.

I can't fight for my mother if she doesn't want to fight for herself or for me, for that matter. Our relationship should not be one-sided. I only help people if they want to help themselves. I only invest in what you truly want for yourselves. I will only take action if I can see a dedication and a willingness to work toward your growth on your end, too. This is my golden rule with my mother and in all of life—especially in coaching.

MY FOSTER FAMILY

Around the age of twelve, I went to live with a new foster family. The foster mother was a teacher and the foster father had a good, stable career in accounting. This led my aunt to believe that they would be able to provide for me in ways she couldn't especially since I desperately needed help with my education and speech. For the first time in my life, I had some actual stability. I had parents. I had a family again. I had a mom to do makeup with and buy me my first doll. She was the perfect mother and he was the dream dad, teaching me sports like softball and cross-country running and going camping and fishing together.

When I moved in, my foster parents sat me down and let me know that I could confide in them about anything and that I was now a part of their family. I was ecstatic to finally have parents like this in my life. Parents I could safely care about and who would openly embrace me. This was so good for me; it was what I had dreamed of.

Several years later, they legally adopted me! I was incredibly happy that I had finally found a home and a family I could call my own. How amazing—I, a fourteen-year-old-teenager, got adopted (not many teenagers get adopted) and had a real shot at happiness!

But before the adoption, I started to see signs that they were like everybody else that I'd believed in and depended on. I was so blinded by my gratitude to finally be somewhere I could call home, though, that I didn't speak up. Originally, I saw very committed, loving, stable parents. Then, when I was in high school, my adoptive parents' attitude seemed to change. But the bad still wasn't a truth that I was ready to accept.

I saw that they were uncommitted, had serious problems they were deeply immersed in, and had insecurities that greatly affected their lives and mine. I felt like they'd lied and used me like everyone else had. They were not who they said they were. Devastatingly, the honeymoon phase had come to a close, and they'd shown me their true colors and I'd shown them mine. This was not a good sight for either of us to see; we weren't treating each other with respect anymore.

At this point, I probably started my self-sabotaging patterns and building my protective walls. I wonder if I gave them my full trust or only the amount I felt I could safely give at the time. I believed that I probably had one foot out the door and one foot in the relationship, as I was taught to do throughout my life. I know that my emotions were a lot for me and others to handle at the time—I had tons of anger and other pent-up emotions that were probably released on them. I know I wasn't the perfect angel, but I loved them and gave them my heart.

They later adopted another child (this time an infant named Drew), which, of course, I was very excited about. I was going to be a big sister again and I would have the opportunity to connect with him and watch him grow up.

However, I gradually felt like I was becoming the Cinderella of the house. There were often stipulations and conditions about having free time for myself. If we wanted to hang out together, Drew and I had to do their laundry, babysit, do yardwork, and fix up the house (take down popcorn ceilings, etc.). I knew it was wrong, but I was still so grateful to finally have a home and I wanted to be with my new baby brother.

My time with them only lasted about five years. Though it had started out as a fairy tale, everything changed for the worst. Taylor and I often wonder what it would have been like if we had hired a Life Coach like me. We think we might have had a happy family because we all needed just a little more help.

They had different views from what they had originally told me. The whole "confide in them" speech was no longer valid. I felt like they were two-faced and did not keep their word. The conditions only got worse, becoming so bad that I moved/was kicked out and, of course, I felt like I was losing another family, brother, and home. They wouldn't let me take my belongings or the car that I'd paid for myself. I didn't even get to say good-bye to my baby brother.

I felt bad that I was leaving yet another brother behind, but they didn't even try to stop me. This is what broke my heart and fragile trust the most. It was clear to me that they were relieved. All I wanted was for them or, for that matter, anyone to try for me, to be there for me, and to love me unconditionally for who I was. I wanted good memories that I would want to look back on, memories that would make me smile. I have a couple of them, but obviously, good memories are not at all I ended up with.

Being left behind was yet another experience I had become far too familiar with. Each family I started to fall in love and felt at home with eventually turned me away. I still had no one!

I knew that my adoptive parents had the best intentions when they adopted me, but in this case, that was not enough. They made a difference in my life. It is hard to describe how. The main gift they gave me was my cousins, aunts, and uncles, who I still have today. I will always be grateful for that and everything that went down in those five years. But I thank God that they were not my permanent family.

My Forever Family

Thankfully, I met Taylor, and as soon as we started dating, I knew deep in my heart that he was the man I would marry! I really did know that right away. Is that crazy? When I met his parents, I was simply in awe of them. They showed me unconditional love from the get-go and they still do, always and forever. They had rules and boundaries, but all of them were loving guidance, which was something I was unfamiliar with because I had never received it before. I was so unfamiliar with this kind of love that I started to sabotage myself and my new relationship with the Ehricks, but luckily, they didn't let me.

At the age of seventeen, I had the life-changing opportunity to move in with the them, and I finally found my permanent, dream family. It took tons of work to get to the point where I trusted that this was *my* reality. Taylor (bless his heart) gave me his room, and he slept on the couch for several years. I was so grateful to be living with a real, honest, loving, giving family that had no hidden agenda.

Taylor and his family taught me so much about the unconditional love of God and that when you have faith, *He* leads your path in the right direction. I was finally worth loving, in someone else's eyes. It was amazing to allow my new parents and God to carry me when I needed it because I knew that I could trust all of them and Him.

In those few years of living with the Ehricks, I learned about healthy beliefs and routines, how to be an optimistic person, and, most important, how to be a valued member of a true, healthy, functioning family. The Ehricks continue to parent me and support me in my life as though I am their very own because, to them, I am. Taylor and his family helped shape me into the wonderful, powerful, trusting woman I am today.

The pain of my life gave me the opportunity to triumph and find my place in this world. For that, I will always have a sense of gratitude toward God. He gave me the gift of my pain and suffering, and it made me who I am today.

2

WHAT CHANGED MY WHOLE LIFE

MY GIFT FROM GOD, TAYLOR

Taylor and I met in the big, scary high school lunchroom on my first day at my brand-new school. I was a fifteen-year-old sophomore and he was a seventeen-year-old senior. I was terrified because I had never been in a school as large as this one or seen that many kids in one place. I was shocked and overwhelmed; to me it looked like how I imagined a college campus would because of the sheer amount of people, eating choices, and possibilities to get lost. I didn't know anyone there. Having grown up in the middle of nowhere, I found the size of the school intimidating in and of itself. Thankfully, when benevolent Taylor saw me standing by myself, looking lost, he nervously swaggered over to me and asked if I would like his chair and if I wanted to sit with him and his friends.

After that magical, memorable moment, we became friends rather quickly. We started going to sporting events like basketball and football games and taking part in school activities. He began coming to my volleyball games to support me, too. I'm pretty sure he thought I was beautiful from the first time he saw me in the lunchroom, and I know he wanted to start dating right away. It took me from September to February to see that I had the perfect guy right in front of me.

One afternoon after a basketball game (his favorite sporting events to go to), I asked him if he was going to ask me out already and when we were going to be boyfriend and girlfriend.

We started dating right after that. He was the sweetest, nerdiest guy I could have ever asked God for. He was so different from anyone else I had ever met. He was so pure and genuine, not to mention unique. I asked him to the Sadie Hawkins dance, which was the first of many fun school dances we spent together. He dressed up as a cowboy—he had a big truck, so, he was already a cowboy in my mind—and we had a wonderful time. The next school dance was homecoming, and, of course, we went together because we both loved to dance. Taylor even came to my senior prom, as a sophomore in college, to ensure I would have the full high school experience. I will forever cherish the memories we made together back then and the new ones we are making together now.

In high school, our first official date was when he cooked for me. He made *chicken alfredo*, my favorite meal at the time. He even got permission to use his parents' pool house. It was so romantic and yummy. I remember the candles and how shocked I was that he could cook. He truly went above and beyond for me.

After dating for two years, we took a trip to his parents' ranch, and while watching the sun set over the beautiful mountains of northern Arizona, he proposed! I was only seventeen and he was nineteen.

Naturally, all the adults in our life were concerned about our getting engaged at such a young age, but we were (and still are) in love, true love! Although, we were young, we did not intend to get married for multiple years and wanted to wait until Taylor graduated from college and I completed cosmetology school. We also needed to save money to make our wedding dreams come true.

When we started dating, Taylor, being as sweet as he is, invited and took me to church. That's how we met Pastor Joe, who'd known me when I was fifteen and had known Taylor as a little boy. We were so blessed that this pastor married us. Taylor and I were married at the Prescott Resort in Arizona, overlooking the city of Prescott and the valleys to the north where I had spent so much time growing up. It was such a beautiful day that I cannot find the words to do it the justice it deserves.

When we got married, I was just twenty and Taylor was twenty-two. I was blessed to have Taylor's dad walk me down the aisle. He helped shape me into the person I am today during those formative years when I lived with the Ehrick family. I was honored and overjoyed to have a dad in my life. It felt so safe, real, and magical.

When I started to float down the aisle with Taylor's dad by my side, the wind picked up to an incredible speed. It was so windy that my veil began to float in front of me clouding my ability to see where I was walking. After a couple of seconds of dealing with my veil, I made the split-second decision to gracefully rip the veil out of my hair and throw it. This made Papa Bear and I crack up laughing. This is a memory neither of us will ever forget.

As I continued down the aisle, my heart started to melt when I saw that everyone I loved was there to share this special day with Taylor and me. And when I saw Taylor standing there so handsome at the end of the aisle with our supportive pastor and my three cute and amazing five- and six-year-old cousins and our ring bearer and our flower girl, my eyes swelled up with tears because I knew I was marrying my forever partner. I knew this would be the best day of my life. I'd been enamored of him instantly because of his genuine disposition and his sweet personality. I was able to trust him completely, securely knowing he would never hurt me. On our wedding day, I knew, I just knew, that we would be together forever.

Our wedding was beautiful. It was a fairy tale and my dream come true. We loved that we were now married, and we were blissfully happy, finally starting our life together. We were on top of the world! We had the best adventures planned for our new beginning. Taylor had received a full-ride scholarship to the University of California-Berkeley, so our plan for our first year of being Mr. and Mrs. Ehrick was to live in Berkeley. How cool it was to dream of living there—exploring, learning, and being together. Wow were we lucky! We had a multitude of dreams and big plans.

MY PERMANENT PARTNER FOR LIFE

Shortly after we were married, I walked into a hospital as a retired twenty-year-old volleyball athlete who worked out daily and was pretty healthy overall for a simple outpatient procedure that did not go as planned and led to a thirty-day struggle spent mostly in the intensive care unit.

I want to describe to you the intensity of the surgeries I chose to have and what became one of the most difficult times of my life. The surgeries changed my life completely and transformed who I was and who I would become. The instant they finished the procedure, it felt as though my entire body began to fight the surgery. In the recovery room, I quickly began to sense that something wasn't quite right. I was supposed to stay at the hospital that first night merely for observational purposes, but with the first meal, I began throwing up and could not keep down any food, which, at the time, wasn't a natural occurrence for me.

Over the next several days, my condition continued to decline drastically. I could not convince anyone around me that something felt severely wrong. I didn't know what it was—I just knew something felt not right. The pain was excruciating, and I begged God, *please just take me home to You and let me be free from this pain.*

Finally, the doctors took some scans, and when the results came back, I was immediately rushed to the operating room. The life altering scans revealed that my stomach had perforations, causing stomach fluid along with infection to spread throughout my entire body. The doctors patched my stomach where it had perforated, and I woke up in the ICU again.

It turned out that my stomach had somehow twisted around inside me to the point that it was cutting off circulation to my small intestines and possibly causing damage to my vagus nerve. Later that week, I underwent my third surgery in three weeks to address my twisted stomach. I was on the operating table for several hours as the doctors completely opened me up and tried to the best of their ability to return all of my internal organs to the way they were before the very first surgery. I was crushed and devastated when I realized that all this pain and suffering had been for what felt like no reason.

Afterward, I was placed on a ventilator to help control my breathing and keep my body in a relaxed state so I could get some rest. I had been through so much that my body couldn't handle anymore, and I was worried about the addition of more issues to my life when I already had so much emotional damage to work through.

I woke up with tubes down my throat that were crowding my airway—the system that was meant to assist my breathing made me feel as if I were suffocating. My arms were tied to the bed, no one else was in the room, and I felt lost and confused from the medication. I had absolutely no control; I was stuck lying there helpless, alone, and afraid. I cannot describe the terror that I felt as I awoke to an empty room, in that condition. That truly nerve-racking feeling still haunts me to this day.

After my long stay in the ICU and several more days of recovery from multiple surgeries, I was released from the hospital with a stapled stomach and tons of baggage to add to my suitcase of problems. I had a TPN (total parenteral nutrition) line in my arm because there was no other way to receive nutrition. I was trying to grasp the idea that my world had turned upside down, and I was unable to see any future for myself.

I spent the greater part of the next year in and out of doctors' offices and hospitals and labs being intensely studied and tested in hopes of figuring out how to manage my health situation. All this while my new husband was working toward his master's degree in transportation engineering at Berkeley (one of the top schools for his field). Over the next ten months, I discovered that I my stomach and bowels had severe gastroparesis, meaning my food digested at a very slow rate. The more complex the food is to break down, the more slowly the stomach and bowels will move and the harder they have to work to process the food. I could no longer eat solid foods or drink anything without throwing up.

Over time, my condition worsened to the point where I had to have a feeding tube inserted through my nose, so I could get the nutrition I needed to survive. I also had to take an excruciatingly terrible test run to find out if I was a candidate for a permanent feeding tube. A plastic nasogastric tube that went down my nose, through my throat and all the way to my stomach. This nasogastric (NG) tube rubbed on my nose making my naval cavity painfully raw. There was bleeding along with coughing. It was miserable! The tubes coming in and out of me terrified children, and the tube hurt me physically and emotionally. It was so awful that I wouldn't wish it on my worst enemy.

I had been throwing up meals and getting by on very little nutrition for several months. I was in my prime with a fantastic healthy, womanly figure, and now here I was, down fifty pounds from my wedding day and having lost all my beautiful, feminine curves. I lost my figure, my whole physique! I was quite miserable, and I had been consumed by my loss and unimaginable pain. The thud that my helpless body made when it hit rock bottom could have been heard in the middle of a raging rock concert.

In a period of less than six months, I had experienced the entire rainbow of emotions, from the ultra-high of getting married and starting a new life with my husband, to the unexpected, instantaneous fall of losing my health forever. At this point, the self-doubt started to creep in, causing me to start to deeply worry about what my new fight would be like and how it would affect my life. I began feeling guilt about ruining my family's lives and my husband's life, too. I tried to push away everyone who was trying to help me, as far away as possible, so they wouldn't get hurt like I was hurt. This didn't work out in my favor.

As I mentioned before, my genius husband lived in another state and although we talked on skype daily, I couldn't help but feel that he was living "our" life while I was living someone else's. Poor Taylor was my life coach, helping me to heal, one insecurity at a time.

My massive health problems were super difficult to deal with at the time and made me very needy. We (Taylor and I) had to constantly make huge decisions—via Skype—about my health and where to go next. I was so scared of having to make all these choices and facing all these life changes that were happening to us. My health issues took up so much of my God-sent husband's time and patience. I was so lucky to have him then and I still am. We weren't discussing or focusing on what normal couples where talking about, like getting a dog or starting a family. We were talking about feeding tubes, surgeries and health care issues.

Then, in the spring of 2011, I began seeing two very talented doctors whose primary goals were to keep me alive and give me a life worth fighting for. I underwent my fourth surgery ten months after the original surgery. The best thing I can compare it to, for understanding purposes, is a gastric bypass surgery. It involved the insertion of my permanent feeding tube into my small intestines. This surgery definitely was not because I needed to lose weight, it was so I could receive the nutrients I so desperately needed to survive and so that I could keep something in my stomach without it rotting or causing me to vomit. I'd made the only, but difficult decision to have this done so I could get this permanent feeding tube to try to live as normal a life as possible.

During the first several months of having my new tube, I could only shower/bathe with one hand (and the help of Taylor's kind mother) because initially the feeding tube could easily fall out of my body—just one of many examples of how my tube affected my newlywed lifestyle. My feeding tube had become my *other* permanent partner.

I am now able to drink certain liquids through my mouth, which I am very thankful for. And I can take a daily liquid formula (through my feeding tube) that increases my chances of getting the proper amount of nutrients and calories. Even though it is all through a machine that I have to carry on my back and a permanently inserted feeding tube, both attached to me 24/7, I am still happy to be alive.

Because I chose my tube just ten months after I married Taylor, my feeding tube became my new permanent partner, too. All in the same moment, not only did I lose myself on this path, but I lost my mother to drugs and the streets again.

Our Journey of Extending Our Family

The only things that saved us during this journey were God's grace and the unconditional love and support that our families freely gave us.

After Taylor completed his program at Berkeley, we bought our first house—it was wonderful. I was so proud of us because we were so young; I was just twenty-one and he was twenty-three.

With one dream checked off our list, now it was time to start our perfect dream family we had always wanted. We always dreamed of having one adopted child and one biological child. We tried for quite some time to have a biological child, but we were unsuccessful. Unfortunately, the doctor's conclusion was that my poor health was the reason. The guilt I felt on finding out I could not give my husband a family was immense, intense, and left me feeling incredibly heartbroken.

Ultimately, I was harsh on myself. We made the decision to exhaust all our resources to have a biological family, so we went with In Vitro Fertilization (IVF). I pushed myself and Taylor through multiple rounds of IVF and had success in getting pregnant but staying pregnant was the problem. I remember crying in the garage for hours on end, not knowing how to stop or what I had to live for. IVF is a common way for families to get pregnant, when they are struggling. I still believe in its goodness and have seen IVF work successfully for other families, but I think that in my case it caused some serious hormonal problems, based on how many rounds I pushed myself through and how hard I had to fight in such a short period of time. I really wanted a child to love, nurture, hold, and call my own. I can only imagine what IVF did to my poor body, which was already in crummy health. We prayed and pleaded, asking God to please give us the child we wanted with every fiber of our being. We had such high hopes each time but no success. This left us with lost dreams and painful memories.

The stipulations and limits put on our daily lives and sexual life were also extreme. Add in the depletion of our bank account, and life seemed impossible and our dreams were so far out of reach. These years were extraordinarily devastating, and for what? We had nothing to show for it except emotional scars. Our fragile hearts couldn't take much more loss or pain. We didn't give up though. Looking back at this whole process, I am grateful for what I learned, but I know this wasn't the time that I was meant to be a mother.

Switching gears, we jumped into adoption. We went through all the state training and made it abundantly clear that we did not want to foster an unadoptable child. One afternoon I got a call from a social worker about a baby boy who was very healthy and available for adoption, so I called Taylor, and without any hesitation we agreed to take in this beautiful child and love him as our very own. Our child would have the dream family that I'd always longed for.

That was the day I got to be a mom for the first time and Taylor got to be a dad. It was such a beautiful feeling for both of us and our families. The boy was eleven months old, already walking and as cute as can be. It was the best gift in the world to have this little boy in our family. We were so grateful to him for making our house into a home.

Things were difficult the first couple of months, though. He had all kinds of sleeping and behavioral problems, but he soon started to really change and found safety and love with us.

Shortly thereafter, we were required to meet with his social worker for a routine check-in, and to our devastation, we were informed that he was, in fact, not on the list for adoption. We also learned that his mom was still fighting for him and that it would only be a matter of time before we lost our child. This was so heartbreaking because we had made it so clear that we didn't want to foster a child because we knew we could never give a child up, and here we were having to do just that.

So, after almost a year of dealing with the "system," plans were made to give the newest addition to our family back to his "druggy" mom. If she hadn't been doing drugs and other unsafe and inappropriate things, we would have supported giving him back, but that wasn't the case.

At that point, I lost it. I hit a new rock bottom and I brought my marriage down with me.

I knew this chapter of my life needed to be closed. I knew I needed someone to help me work through all the awful pain and hurt. So, I found a therapist to help me figure out what I should do next.

After meeting with her, I made a plan to put our little boy into a temporary foster home, a home with parents who wouldn't get attached to him like we did. The pain of the upcoming separation was suffocating me and eating me alive. That day was the same day that the therapist told me, I should be doing what she is doing and that I needed to go to school to become a therapist. I found him a better-suited foster home, one with parents who had the experience and ability to let children go, something I could never do. Sadly, that little boy has been in and out of foster care ever since. To this day, I don't understand state policies. I just wanted what was best for our little boy. I wanted him to live in a good, safe home where he had consistent love. I knew that he had a hard life ahead and he would be bounced around from one house to another, just like I was, and I could no longer be part of a system that was always giving children back to biological parents who'd been labeled unfit in the first place! I often wonder whose best interests were the greatest factor, the children's or the parents'.

Fortunately, because Taylor and I were so in love and so committed to each other and our marriage, neither one of us could give up on everything we'd built. We have been together since 2006, twelve years as of 2018! We still do not have a child, which is difficult for us every single day, but we are thankful for each other, and we love our lives together. Our marriage is not perfect by any means, but we are happy with everything we have, and we love our lives. Of course, we would be ecstatic for a new addition of a child to out family, but more than anything, we are grateful for the gift that God has given us, each other.

When two strong, dedicated people are committed to each other, they always try to meet in the middle and work things out. This is why God sent Taylor to me. Taylor is my rock and he is always there for me no matter what, without judgment, and he has proved this to me time and time again, through everything we have been through. I work to be supportive of him, too. By supporting each other, we continue building and nurturing our relationship.

He is the most logical man I have ever met. I, on the other hand, am the complete opposite; I am extremely emotional. We balance each other out almost perfectly. We are like yin and yang; you can't have one without the other. We both work hard on our relationship and keep our communication honest, respectful, and open with the raw truth. I like to think of our marriage as a commitment to my best friend, my partner, my lover, and my incredible gift from God! I work to not have those unrealistic romantic fantasies about relationships, because the truth is you never know what life will throw your way. Taylor and I strive to only see each other in the moment and not in terms of what we have done to each other in the past. I no longer self-sabotage our relationship or fixate on the problems. We no longer assume we know what each other is thinking or feeling. We look for ways to understand each other as individuals and not only support but meet each other's needs.

We also strive to respect and love each other for exactly who we are. We bring out the best in/of each other. I've stopped asking him to be who I wanted him to be. And I stopped pushing him to define our relationship. We share our insecurities and fears with each other. We work through our problems as a team, and we let go as a couple. Our relationship is two-sided.

All these methods we use with each other are the reason we are still together today and get along so well. We bring out the best in each other.

My Daily Routine

Today when people see me, all they perceive is a strong, healthy, and confident young woman, inspiring by speaking and coaching with the help of God. This is totally me and I love that people see that about me. However, what most don't know about me is how I am actually feeling and all I am going through with my medical condition. I used to wish people could see this internal truth, my true physical pain, but now I realize that my pain would be too much of a burden for others to see. And because they cannot see it, my inner-pain, I can do my work of healing people and helping people to do *their* work.

I do this no matter how distracting my pain is. My health has given me purpose and a drive. The pain drives my work in my practice and reminds me that life is worth living with whatever cards I am dealt. We are all dealt the cards of life to play with; how we want to play our cards is our choice.

Most people spend the first part of their morning with a cup of coffee and a big bowl of cereal, maybe watching a little news on TV. Some make a huge family breakfast on the weekends, while others go for a hike or a jog. When *I* get up every morning, my body is already physically exhausted due to lack of nutrition and hormone imbalances and the workload that my constant crummy condition puts on my body. I also get to wake up with nausea every single morning.

After I deal with all of that for a period of time, I have gained the discipline to start the process of hooking up to my feeding tube, which I know means taking on more nausea and dry heaving. When I tell someone I am hooking up, I don't mean it in the popular sense of the phrase, as my family likes to joke. I literally mean I am hooking up to feed myself. With my measuring cup, I put in the feed, my supplements (five to ten different types), and then add in antibiotics/probiotics and whisk with bone broth to thin the mixture so it can flow through the small tube—I feel like Julia Child! Next, I pour the concoction into the bag attached to my machine and tube, which I put in my backpack. Then I must insert that tube into my permanent feeding tube attachment that is in my stomach. After that, I tape around the end of the tube for safety and anti-infection purposes. This allows me to hug and have other physical contact with others and to play with or touch my dogs. This whole process is necessary for me to be able to "eat."

Between meals, I must flush my tubes with water. I do this every two to three hours throughout the day, seven days a week, 365 days a year. Unlike with my coaching career, I do not get any days off from this time-consuming process!

When I leave the house, I can't just grab my keys, phone and purse and go. No, I have to make sure I pack my three different formulas, my medications, my vitamins, extra tubes, bandages, tape, extra clothing (for accidents/leaks), my measuring cup, and much more. All of this must go with me wherever I go, whether I'm just going to the store for ten minutes or heading out for a full-day speaking event. My family members have told me it's easier to get young children out the door than it is to get myself out the door. And at the end of the day, I'm still not off the hook. Before bed, instead of just grabbing a good book to read, I have to go through a whole other process, unhooking, cleaning, and preparing for the next day.

Malfunctions with the bag, pump, and attachments are another regular part of life. The equipment can and does malfunction quite often and when they happen I have to be prepared (as best I can) to fix the problem immediately. Trying to get new equipment of any kind is another hassle with this system of procedures. Being on the phone with the insurance company is not only agonizing, stressful, and difficult but it is often disappointing. When they can't deliver equipment in a timely manner, which is always the case, I am forced to either go through excruciating pain to try to eat orally or starve myself. Gee, what great choices! Sometimes I go three or four days without eating, which leaves me very weak, tired, and disoriented. When I must eat orally, I have to force myself to eat. And then there are times when I just go crazy and want to taste food and be normal. In either case, I must cowboy up to the consequences that I'm going to face after eating or not eating.

Machines dictate my day and I have no alternative options. This, my health, and I have learned to let go of control. I take a deep breath and accept the situation I'm facing. I live in the moment and focus on my health at the times it is required of me. Loving what I have, I do not look to the future. When malfunctions happen during my professional day as a Life Coach, it is a beautifully messy learning experience for me and those around me; I am grateful that I have learned that messiness is a good thing. My clients know that working with me means that my permanent partner may beep or malfunction. They are so kind and understanding, and together we just go with the flow.

I also have to constantly be aware of my "accessories"—my backpack and tubes—especially when I bend over. If the backpack hits me in the back of the head, the tubing may get air in it, which then causes an error with the machine, which in turn causes a nagging beeping. I have to be careful when I sit down or even walk around to ensure that the cords do not get caught on anything or anyone for that matter. Don't even get me started on the struggle with public restrooms. There are tubes everywhere and they are touching everything; this causes complications, especially if there is no pursue hook in the stall. The tubes are particularly annoying because they are in my pants and consist of sharp objects that push against me all day. When errors occur like tubes getting pinched or some other problem occurs, I get to hear beeping comparable to an obnoxious car alarm. I have to be very careful because I only have one aperture that can be used for my tubes, and it often gets sore and sometimes infected. The tubes always have to be considered, and my bag has to always be in the upright position. With that being said, imagine how sexy I look and how awkward our intimate activities are with all my unique "accessories."

There are times when unexpected things happen, and I am forced to go to the hospital due to infections, malfunctioning of the permanently attached feeding tube, etc. Sometimes those hospital visits become another surprised, unplanned procedure or surgery.

When engaging in most daily activities or chores I love to do must be constantly monitored to ensure that all my accessories are in place. I love creating and doing new projects with my husband, such as building furniture and remodeling the RV, but sometimes I just can't be a part of those activities because my bag and tubes are in the way. There are so many variables, and it changes day to day.

My wonderful husband has built and installed all kinds of support mechanisms around our home to make my life easier as I carry around this backpack so that the tubes don't get caught up in anything. There are hooks all over for hanging my backpack and medical poles, as well as a built-in medical station in our bedroom. I could go on and on about all the great things he has done and made for me.

Outside our home, my activities are limited, as the places we go need to accommodate me and my many accessories. I can't go swimming in lakes or public pools. Plane trips are hardest of all because I am not randomly picked for body search—I'm always searched because of the equipment that has to stay on me at all times. It's almost shameful being publicly patted down. However, the upside of flying is that we get to pre-board. Taylor and his brother think that's just greatest!

When opportunities arise that I am unable to participate in, I turn to my hugging machines, my two beautiful Saint Bernards that were trained by my talented trainer friend and power partner Cathy Dolan. They were trained specifically to ensure that their big lovable bodies don't get tangled in my tubes. They also help me release any emotions I may have due to the stress of my imperfect health.

Even though my husband and Drs. Michelle Retz and Jonathan (Jake) Psenka of Longevity Medical Center and the team at the Mayo Clinic have helped me with my health and my tubes, which has made life a bit easier for me, I still deal with a multitude of daily problems. People ask me all the time, "Is it still hard for you to not be able to eat normally like other people?" And my answer is "Of course it's still hard for me!" It's our animal instinct and our human nature to crave food and the need to eat food! I'm also asked what my formula tastes like, and I respond that I do not know; it goes through my bowel, not my mouth. I can't taste it.

It's awkward to sit there and watch everyone else eat their helpings of food or make a toast with their glasses filled with a wine that pairs nicely with the meal they are eating. At family events and social outings, there is always eating and drinking. I miss that aspect of my social life. It's hard at family events when my four-year-old niece looks up at me and asks, "Why don't you have a plate, Auntie?" I have to sit back and say Auntie is unique and the way I eat is different. I don't want to tell her how crazy hungry I really am.

My actual oral intake of regular food is very complex to the point my doctors and I don't even understand. However, under very special and extenuating circumstances I am able to eat orally, in very small amounts, though I can never have alcohol. Unfortunately, it does come with side effects of pain, nausea, bloating, and then vomiting. The aftermath of it all in the bathroom; I will spare you the details! The process of being able to eat is so complex and constantly changing; I can't keep up and neither can my bowels. I ask that you never try to understand my health; it's impossible. I just live in the moment giving my body what it needs. I don't get to question the process either. I tried questioning and understanding for a very long time and it did me no good.

I used to do most of the food shopping for our household, which was difficult as the smell of poultry in the stores is very nauseating for me. I made the majority of these beautiful meals for my husband and I do my best to enjoy the smells and the process of cooking, but it is much different than it used to be, when I could enjoy my hard work, too. Another downside to not being able to taste the food, is I have no clue if it tastes any good. I just have to watch Taylor's face when he takes the first bite, wondering what the food tastes like. As far as our "date nights", it's different because Taylor's ideal date would be to go out for a nice dinner. Because of this, we have gotten very creative with our adventures and outings. We enjoy them, even though at times, we still deal with the disappointment of not being able to do many of the things we used to be able to do together. Now, Taylor and I grocery shop together because I tend to forget important tasteful ingredients necessary for a good home-cooked meal. I now understand that things worth achieving don't come quickly or easily and can be incredibly painful. I know my misery is a choice, even though I have to endure the pain. But if we take the time to unwrap the gift of the lesson you are meant to learn you will find the gift you are meant to uncover and receive.

3

How Far I've Come

What I Had to Let Go of to Become a Life Coach

Although I didn't know that something was preventing me from growing and being happy and at peace, I had a serious case of hidden emotions that I did not recognize until I became a Life Coach. For so long, I lived in total self-doubt, I had no self-confidence, I always questioned everything, and I had oodles of insecurities.

I know that a lot of people hide from their pain. As for me, I never hid from it. I always wanted a solution to the uneasy feeling I had in my gut. I couldn't help feeling that I wasn't living my life to the fullest. In the moment, all I knew was that something was missing. Though I felt like my life was pretty good because I had come so far compared with everybody else in my family, I was missing freedom from my thoughts and my self-sabotaging patterns. I used to think about what it would be like to truly be happy and fill the void. I always thought the void was not having my own child, not having finished college, or some other form of unfulfillment. What I now know is that the void was all my stress, baggage, planning, and worries. The void was basically me playing games in my head, especially the "what if" game. Whenever I played, I somehow ended up losing. I was constantly worried about what people thought about me. I wasn't living in the present moment even though I thought I was. I wasn't truly enjoying life's gifts. I had no clue how precious and valuable they are. I am lucky that I know now.

Money was super-tight, and I had a horrible relationship with money anyway. I believed money would give me safety, a sense of security, and happiness. When I didn't have enough income, I would go crazy with overbearing thoughts and fear of the unknown. I gave funds (or lack thereof) so much control over me, again totally unaware that I was giving away my power. My past had taught me to have a poor mind-set, and I didn't realize how hard it is to change that.

I lived in a world of pure fear. I was scared of everything and everyone. I worried about what could happen to me, what *was* happening to me and what had *already* happened to me. Fear ate me up inside. Fear drove me through my life. I had so much stress and the only way I knew how to deal with all my stress was by living on autopilot, just to survive.

I tried to control everything I did. I planned out every single waking minute of my life. I would do anything to stay busy, unaware that it was a coping mechanism, a mask I wore to keep me from having to look at my pain and my real-life problems. I lived a life filled with distractions and busy work. I lacked self-love when it came to my internal self-talk, as well and I didn't put my health first. I always put my husband and my career before my own needs and wants. I didn't know who I was, and I became my own worst enemy. Every word I spoke about and to myself was self-destructive and constantly negative. I would always compare myself with others, which creates unhealthy competition. Be as beautiful as you are. Be bold to impress yourself. Be you because you are the only *you*. These are now words I live by.

At the time, I let people stomp all over me, take advantage of me, and use me until I became a doormat. I preferred to be nice and accommodating rather than causing any sort of confrontation. I was secretly, a very angry and frustrated person living behind the facade of a happy, servile person, which only made my life worse. I would become increasingly upset because I would hold everything in until I exploded with uncontrollable extraordinary outbursts directed at my husband. I never had a clue why I was so angry. I could never recognize my own anger because I didn't want to be angry like my mother or her boyfriends. I thought angry people were bad. I now know that anger isn't a bad emotion; it's all about how you use it and project it.

I felt I was not good enough for anyone, not even for myself, and that feeling was controlling my life making me feel helpless. I continued to play it "safe" because "safe" was easier or, so I thought. Because I went through all of my many limiting health issues, unsuccessful IVF (leaving me with no children), and everything in my chaotic childhood, I felt as though I had nothing to live for. I had no passion, no purpose. I had no faith or trust in myself, and there were even times when I doubted my faith or lost it altogether.

All I wanted to do was use my pain to help others. I didn't realize that my pain was still suffocating me and that I was trapped, unable to seize the opportunities in front of me. I felt so defeated and useless. Once I became a Life Coach, I knew that the only way to be successful was to be humble and love myself, but what I didn't know was how.

It was so bad that I couldn't even take a compliment. I would deflect the kind, thoughtful words every time. A perfect example was when Taylor would tell me I looked gorgeous and perfect the way I was, and I would argue with him, saying I was fat and ugly. This would shut him down and make him feel frustrated. I was so sensitive to every word people said and the way they treated me. Don't even get me started on the expectations I had for people and how they should treat me and everyone else. My expectations crept into my relationships and my life in general, causing more deeply rooted problems.

All of this built up to the point where I was like a ticking time bomb, trying to please everyone. Tick... Tick... Tick... Tick! Ready to explode because I was unaware of my emotions and feelings. My emotional bomb would explode on anybody and everybody close to me.

When I think back to who I was, I can see that the biggest game changers were my relationship and, of course, getting my freedom. I had thought Taylor was the one who needed to change and grow, but what I hadn't thought about before I became a Life Coach was that I was the one who need to change and grow. I thought I was changing, but I had no idea what growth was or how much hard work it took. I thought I was changing, but it wasn't enough. At that point in time, I needed to figure out who I was; I needed to find my freedom the healthy way. The funny but painful thing was that Taylor was the conscious, present partner, patiently waiting for me to grow and share our lives together. He was already emotionally mature, just sitting and waiting there for me; the waiting and my self-sabotaging cycle caused him to lose faith and trust, and love in our relationship. He watched me throw emotional fits and create drama because I wasn't emotionally mature enough.

I was accustomed to feeding off of unhealthy energy. Unhealthy energy was about the only thing that remained consistent throughout my life. I had no clue that I'd been trapped in insanity the whole time. I was the type of girlfriend/wife who would demand change in a way that would make Taylor feel as though he would never be good enough. I would strip him down to nothing and push him to be my mirror because I thought that he needed to be emotional like me for us to be happy. I would unknowingly coach him—harshly—to change and grow. I am so grateful that I learned that that behavior was unhealthy for our relationship and our sanity. Our relationship today is calm, peaceful, and fun; we both worked really hard to obtain this.

I told you this story about my husband and me because now that I'm in my healthy permanent patterns, I can't even imagine going back. One of the most difficult things for me to do was to forgive everybody who has been in my life, the people who have hurt me, abandoned me, and the people who have done wrong by me. This is something I had to do to become a successful Life Coach and to walk the talk in my practice. Some people were more difficult to forgive than other, but nevertheless, I did it. I made the choice to forgive the people who needed to be forgiven, and I continue to forgive people every day. Sometimes forgiveness is for both parties. I had to learn to forgive myself as well. Forgiveness can release almost everything. Forgiveness is a very powerful tool. Don't hesitate to use it. I never do.

CERTIFICATIONS

I knew that getting my certifications would be its own journey. I knew it would be very difficult. To be completely honest, I was terrified. But at the same time, I was excited. I am so grateful to all of my teachers, who helped me gain my certifications.

I enrolled in one of the top accredited coaching programs in the United States, with the most difficult and challenging curriculum I could find: The Institute for Professional Excellence in Coaching (iPEC) to become a Life Coach to help others who needed the help that I once needed. I remember sitting there, with no voice, as I listened so intently and realized this was what I had been waiting for my whole life. I felt that I belonged there more than anywhere else and that this was going to be the place where I would finally find my purpose.

I overcame some massive fears in that program, building up the courage to ask questions and being able to speak up in front of other people. Before, I'd felt as though I had nothing worthwhile to say and I was terrified of public speaking, even in a classroom setting. But my coaching program gave me a sense of community, thanks to the friends I made there who were like me. This laid the foundation for the wonderful life I have today. I never thought I would meet people who wanted to talk about deep emotions as a way of healing from those emotions, but at iPEC I met my peeps!

What a great career I found, helping others overcome things similar to what I had been through! The first thing I learned was that regardless of age or the nature of the problem(s), people are eager to learn when it means understanding the baggage that holds them back from being their best selves. I learned that in order for me to be the amazing Life Coach I am today, I had to take care of my own personal baggage from my past and present and all of my many issues before being able to coach others. In other words, I had to be my own Life Coach. This work had to be done, before I could even consider helping anyone else with what they needed to work on.

Kerri Myers, my instructor at iPEC, talked about the obstacles she had overcome in her life that had brought her to a place of freedom from those obstacles. It was through her story that I finally realized how much I needed the same freedom that she had achieved. After I graduated from the program, I hired her as my personal coach because I knew she was the perfect partner to instill growth and understanding in my life. I knew she could help me be the powerful, life-changing coach I was destined to be. More important, I hired her to help me achieve the life I'd always dreamed of, a life where I had freedom from my self-sabotaging thoughts. I walked the talk by hiring Kerri.

So, I know exactly what it takes to hire a coach and invest in yourself.

Since then I have attended many programs and workshops to be a Life Coach. I also became a certified Kolbe specialist, which is a business coach who helps people identify their natural gifts and talents. I am certified to serve as a Stephen Minister, which means I am equipped and empowered to give confidential, Christ-centered coaching to people who are hurting, at All Saints Lutheran Church. My certifications also include Energy Leadership Index Master Practitioner and professional coach through ACTP (Accredited Coaching Training Program) and FCCI (Fellowship of Companies for Christ international). Also, I am a certified hypnotherapist through the IACT (International Association of Counselors and Therapists) and, as well as the IMDHA (International Medical and Dental Hypnotherapy Association).

On top of all of my official certifications, I feel like I have been a coach my whole life whether I was aware of it or unconscious to it.

HOW I ACHIEVED MY FREEDOM

I am often asked, "Do you recognize how far you have come and all of the obstacles you have overcome to be here?" My answer is that I definitely recognize my growth and the hard work and dedication it took to get here. What I see most clearly is what I have received from overcoming the obstacles: my freedom. I see all the good it has brought me to find this peace in myself. I am always grateful for the distance I have traveled, and I always acknowledge the obstacles I have overcome. I have no regrets about my life or my choices. What I see after overcoming my many obstacles is me being able to smile from the inside out about the joy, peace, and harmony I have built for myself. Getting to live my life without pain, suffering, and baggage is something I will be grateful for the rest of my life. Now I see myself as the happy person I am, not the heaviness that used to define me. I see the gifts that overcoming my obstacles has brought me: family, friends, memories, laughter, my connections within my relationships, and simply being able to live my life without all the nonsense. I finally get to enjoy being present. I get to make a difference in the world by sharing how I overcame my obstacles so that others can do the same. I get to guide people to be the new them with the lightness that comes with being free.

It is so crazy to look back and see how free I have become. It wasn't something that happened overnight. It took me my whole life to obtain success, sanity, and serenity.

I am grateful to have the wonderful life I have. The events of my childhood—good, bad, ugly, and beautiful—and the surgeries are the building blocks of who I am today. I am blessed that I decided to create the amazingly bright future I am now living. I was fortunate enough to have the opportunity to see both sides of human nature (good and bad), and I chose to embrace the events and difficulties I endured because they led me to be the beautiful person I am today. I finally have the freedom from my baggage that was holding me back from being me in the fullest, most real, and best way imaginable. All of this—my past, the programs I've completed, the emotional challenges, the physical complications I endured, and the real-life clients I have helped—makes me the perfect fit to guide you through this journey of self-discovery and self-worth, helping you find a new perspective on your life and bring out the best in you!

4

THE TRUTH IS ALL
THAT MATTERS

BE A TRUTH TELLER

This section will teach you how to be a truth teller. True is what *you* believe is the truth. The truth is absolute. In our society, you get trapped in telling your true and not the absolute truth. You also learn to do this from watching your parents and family members. This gets you into a lot of trouble. You get caught up in your belief about the truth and not the real truth of what happened. It starts to alter your reality and your ability to see the truth as is, without putting your own spin on it. You know how much trouble you get into when you don't face the truth, say the truth, and stand in the truth. What I am really trying to say is that every time you tell yourself or others something different from the actual pure truth, it becomes more difficult to tell or even remember the truth. This is how unhealthy patterns are created and how some lose themselves.

Where in your life do you tell a "true" story without telling the full truth around your story? Is it in your thoughts? Your feelings? Your actions? What is the result? White lies add up. Lying even just a little is still lying. Where do you tell white lies and know you're doing so? Exaggerating is the equivalent of a white lie—it's still a lie. It's still not the honest truth. Where in your life do you exaggerate? You need to learn the truth about life—how will you face and accept your own truths and share them that way? Where in your life do you need to face hard truths? I encourage you to tell your truth every day and to limit your stories purely to the truth.

Now that you can pinpoint those times that you're telling the true and not the truth, how will you stop exaggerating and start telling the pure truth? What will you do to make sure you are free from telling trues? If you are exaggerating and it's for purposes of a joke or something else fun, just make sure people know that it is for effect.

The response I most commonly get from my clients is "I'll stop doing it." That's a great start. Just stop the pattern. Stand in your truth no matter what the cost. (I'm talking about day-to-day stuff, not life-threatening problems). I know it's hard to face conflict, sadness, and possibly hurting others, but those things should not be more powerful than the good feeling you get from doing and saying the right thing for both parties. You have to make a choice to stand in the truth in all areas of your life; you have to be able to deal with the good and the bad consequences of standing in your truth.

Now that you fully understand the difference between true and truth, what new power do you need to stand in and own? I really just wanted to teach the simple side of true and truth so you can better understand what you need to do when you tell stories. You should always tell the full truth of everything in the most kind and loving way whenever possible. Stand in your truth always and forever.

How You Tell Stories

Any time you share *your* life with someone, you are telling them *your* story, from *your* perspective. It's like a movie and you're the director. You have the ability to project the story you concocted in your subconscious mind to show it to yourself and others can watch it, scene by scene. You're also the star of your movie, and because you're the star, you of course choose the best way for you to play the role.

You may purposely or unconsciously leave out certain details that you may not remember, don't want to share, or are too painful to revisit. Of course, there are a multitude of other reasons that may cause you to leave out details, such as shame, guilt, anxiety, fear, and anger, and many more.

You create *your true* about what happened. Sometimes people tell *their* story to keep them safe, so they don't have to move or grow from the situation that affected them. Other times, people tell their stories so that others will feed them energy; some people crave pity from others and they use their story to get it.

Telling your story is very important. It's also important to always remember that you tell your story from your perspective, based on your past, your fears, your pain, your sorrows, your doubts, and your feelings. You put every emotion and feeling you have into your story, consciously and unconsciously. You tell your story about everything that has ever happened to you, while putting your own spin on it.

When scripting your best story to tell others, you add your own positive spin to everything, especially your own personal character. You may do this to make you look good, feel better, or change what actually happened in your mind.

However, some of my clients do the opposite. If they are the type of the person who over-exaggerates what actually happened, they may dramatize their character's persona and everything that happens to them in their story to a negative extreme.

One day, a client of mine went to a job interview, and one of the questions was something along the lines of "Have you ever worked with special needs children and experienced the type of outbursts they have?" My client exaggerated her story to the extreme positive, saying she specialized in working with special needs children even though she had only babysat them and only a couple of times.

My client told this story because she really needed the job, but it blew up in her face. After she got the job, the special needs children she worked with had outbursts left and right. Not only did this put the children in incredible danger because she didn't know the severity of their needs, but she also put herself, her job, and her integrity at risk as well, not to mention the company she worked for and the job of the person who had interviewed her.

As you can see from her story, because of her small lie and exaggeration, she now has guilt and disappointment in herself, and sadly, she lost her much-needed job.

It's like going to an art show. Say there's a group of people viewing the same picture, but each person has their own idea of what the picture is saying or even of what the picture is meant to be. You'll find that each person's description of that same picture is completely different. Some artists intentionally create art that's abstract, hoping to provoke conversation about the piece. Other artists want their art to be seen their way. Like the art show, remember that it is very difficult to tell your story so that everyone sees it your way. That's why it's important to tell your truth/story the same way every time you tell it. Tell your story so that others can see your painting the way it was painted.

DISCOVER YOUR STORIES

What stories do you tell? What stories do you tell yourself and others that are not true and are over the top, negatively or positively? What stories do you tell that feed your safety? Sometimes you tell stories to shield yourself from growth and the unknown. What stories do you tell to protect others? Most of the time, by protecting someone else, you are hurting yourself. You need to stop telling those stories right now because they are hindering your needed growth. How can you let go of those stories? The best way to do this is by walking in the truth of your story. What stories do you tell that steal negative or positive energy from you? What old stories do you need to create a positive mind frame around? What old stories do you need to stop sharing altogether because they have a connection to bad energy? What story have you told purely as the truth? If you have told a story as the truth, work on creating a pattern for telling the truth all the time, because it feels so good to have what actually happened out there. What stories are you holding back that you need to share to heal yourself and others? How will you share these stories? What stories can you tell with more laughter and happiness? What do you know now about your stories that you didn't know before? How can you incorporate that into your stories right now?

I encourage everybody to pay attention to how they portray their story and how much falsehood you are consciously or unconsciously adding to your story and your character. Try focusing on why you tell your story in this way so that you may tell it as close to exactly how it happened. Also try to focus on why you are telling your story this way. Work on figuring out what it feeds you. I know it can be more engaging, attention-grabbing and entertaining to add the spin to your stories but resist that temptation. Now that you know the power of telling your stories as they happened, be the one person in the world who tells them with love and light and the fullness of the truth and nothing but truth, so help me God.

YOUR LIMITING BELIEFS MATTER

A limiting belief is a thought or belief that *you* believe to be true that is limiting you. You may have created your limiting belief or adopted it from someone else. Other limiting beliefs can also include religious, political, cultural or societal beliefs.

You also take on the personal values of people you know and trust and believe them to be your own. More often than not, you don't even know anything about these values you are taking on. You do this because you don't know what you want or what you believe because you think someone else knows better. But it's crazy to let others determine your beliefs and values—you don't know the why behind someone else's limiting beliefs. They do not have the same meaning for you. It has to be right for you. You don't take the time to see how and what those beliefs mean to you. So, take that time now. You keep the limiting belief or limiting value because it's safer and easier than having to form your own.

If you did take on a belief from someone else, is the belief still true for you today? If you created a limiting belief, is the thought still true for you?

A personal limiting belief that I took on and was able to let go of at iPEC with Kerri was that I would never amount to anything if I didn't go to college; without college, you can never be successful or good enough for anybody. My foster mother, a teacher, taught me this belief. Without intending to, she was using aggressive energy and fear tactics to encourage me to get an education. I am who I am despite graduating college. Thank God I didn't go to college and push myself to be a psychologist, because if I had it would have taken me in the completely wrong direction and I wouldn't be the inspirational life coach I was born to be. Do you see how my foster mother's telling me there was only one way to success and happiness was a limiting belief?

We all have limiting beliefs in our lives holding us back. What limiting beliefs or values do you want to look into to see if they are yours or someone else's? Do you want to keep them or get rid of them? Make a list of all the times you have taken on others' beliefs that limited you and write down all the ones you have created yourself that hold you back from success and happiness. It doesn't matter how old you were when you took them on. Make a plan for how you will let go of each item on the list and why you're letting go of it. Some of them may be deeply rooted in your life. Take as much time as you need to replace the limiting beliefs with your true beliefs.

Stay away from the lure of creating your own limiting beliefs or taking on those of others. Stop the pattern now. Limitlessly believe for yourself. Don't be limited by your beliefs. Instead create your own beliefs. Be proud of them. Own them.

THE TRUTH ABOUT DRAMA

At times you feed off of drama and overreact. You know this feeling as you have felt it before. I know lots of people try so hard not to feed off of drama. There are those who truly want to help others get caught up in the drama temporarily but can detach once they recognize what's actually going on. Many people work to keep drama out of their lives, but it's just so sneaky. They have no clue that they are in a dramatic energy or that they are feeding off of it. Some people unconsciously want the drama to be part of their lives because it fuels their ego and much more. And, of course, there are people who live for drama and are fully aware of it. They need others to join their pity party to make themselves feel valued through empathy or sympathy.

Take a deep breath. Take the moment and think to yourself, *where do I attract drama in my life?* Do you feed off of your own drama and overreact, creating unnecessary chaos to keep you busy? I find that most people who are "into" drama, whether it is their own or others', have underlying emotional pain they do not want to face. Drama will distract you—watch out! Take a minute to think of those dramatic/chaotic times in your life and remember how much energy it took from you. What outcome did you get from it? Was it worth it?

Drama can be taking someone else's dramatic energy and turning it into your own and feeding off of it. You are now allowing it to create drama in your life. It prevents you from looking at your own. It is a huge distraction from your present life and goals. Are you aware you are looking for a distraction? Do you recognize that others' problems are distracting you and keeping you from looking at your own issues? Are you ready to be conscious of your drama and other people's drama? If so, this will give you the chance to live a drama-free life or something pretty close to it. Do everything you can to see everybody else's drama but refrain from getting into it with them. Do yourself a huge favor be aware of the drama you create and stop yourself the moment you recognize it. If you live in your truth, there shouldn't be any drama.

FIND THE TRUTH IN YOUR ASSUMPTIONS

When you make an assumption, you think you know what someone is feeling or thinking. A lot of the time, you assume what people think about you and how they feel toward you. Without having any proof, you turn your assumption into a story. You build up this story in your head, allowing it to have control and power over you. You allow this story to play over and over, causing inner turmoil.

You fear the unknown, which is the most obvious instigator of assumptions. When you fear the unknown, you feed your assumption the fuel it needs to keep the story going. You make your assumptions based on past experiences. But you should always assume your assumptions are wrong. If you don't know whether your assumptions are true or false. Try this crazy approach: ask for the facts!

I want to make something clear. You make assumptions about everything in your life, not just what people think or feel about you. Most people make assumptions about people, but people also make assumptions about their environment and what someone or something will look like, be like, taste like, smell like, or sound like. Assumptions turn into expectations.

As the saying goes, when you assume, you make an *"butt"* out of you and *me*. When you assume, you create a problem between you and another person. Assumptions can cause destruction and devastation. When you assume, you do not give the other person the opportunity to tell you their truth or what they are thinking or feeling. You take all the power away when you do this to yourself and others. When you assume, you steal the energy, the moment, and the potential memories that could have been created. If you are making an assumption, you are probably taking things personally and working it up in your head, making it all about you.

So, stop assuming you know what's best for others and quit believing you know what others are thinking. Don't make assumptions about anything in your life. Be aware of your assumptions because they will whisper sweet stories in your ear and feed you spoonsful of crap. I know you would rather let your mind make an assumption than let your ears hear the truth but ignore those stories.

Assumptions cause many deep-rooted problems in our lives and in our thoughts.

Assumptions break up amazing relationships. They even keep you from seeing opportunities in your relationships, work, and just about everywhere else in your life.

Do you want to stop assuming? If so, here are some questions to get you started, and the rest is up to you. How have your assumptions bitten you in the butt? Are you ready to stop assumptions from happening? Do you recognize the mind patterns that lead you to assume, causing a large problem in your life? How can you work every day to stay present to not assume? How do your assumptions distract you from the truth? How can you avoid getting caught up in thinking you know what others are saying, thinking, or feeling about you? Where in your life have you assumed the worst? Have you ever seen the destructiveness your assumptions bring into your life?

Just ask the other person involved—get to the bottom of it. Paraphrase so that nothing gets lost in translation and so that nothing is left for you to assume. Tell the other person you think you heard them say "blah blah blah" to determine whether you are correct. Don't let your thoughts get in the way of the truth. What are you assuming in your life that you just had an aha moment about? Do you know how good it feels to really hear the other person tell you the truth and to not hear the true from your head?

When this mind pattern tries to get itself back into you head, don't let it. It's not worth it. Stay strong. Enjoy conversations, people, and life.

Now that you are free from your assumptions, you will see life in a totally different way—how it really is. Assumptions can never give you the truth; they can only give you what your mind thinks is the truth.

5

CHANGING YOUR OUTLOOK

REFRAMING

Reframing is a state of mind where you make a conscious decision to step back and look at the bigger picture. It is a tool for putting things in a new perspective. When you are trapped in a moment where you cannot see any options, reframing is a wonderful skill because when you step back you can see everything in a way that empowers you to be more positive about what's happening. I love reframing because it gets you out of the problem for just enough time to give you some form of clarity. Generally, when you have the ability to reframe, you have the chance to take action on something new and change the situation.

One of the most important things to do with your thoughts when you are stressed and have a problem is to step back and reframe. Reframing can help you see how big the stress or problem is or how small it actually is. Reframing is all about doing everything you can to get a new perspective, because once you have that new perspective you can easily eliminate your problem. Don't forget the power of reframing your thoughts and your emotions. Always step back and try to find the bigger picture.

When you're reframing, find your internal bridge to hope. A bridge to hope is a means of getting somewhere emotionally, sometimes crossing over a hurdle to get there. I would encourage you to find out if you have a bridge and what it is. And once you do, even though it may be uncomfortable because you're in the unknown, cross over it. While reframing, it's really cool to tap into this type of energy and see if anything is calling out to you. It's probably your internal bridge wanting to help you.

Look for your inner bridge that's calling out to you! Enjoy the process of reframing. It has given my clients and me so many amazing opportunities.

LABELS/IDENTITY

In our society, we place so much importance on labels and identities. You give other people and yourself labels, and you may hold it up to a different standard. It's all how you look at yourself and others—what you believe to be true about yourself, how you perceive and see yourself in the world.

The identities you hold on to—mother/father, doctor, entrepreneur, athlete—also label who you are. How you hold on to labels and how you use them in your everyday life is important. I would be aware of your labels and how they serve you or if and how they have gotten in your way. See whether a label has protected you or distracted you from bad decisions and whether it has given you a purpose or something to be proud of. The important thing is that you always remember you are more than that label. Yes, it's good to be proud of what you do, but in the big picture, it's the love, kindness, loyalty to a Higher Coach, gratitude, and humility that matter most in being a good person!

For twenty-five years, my client Larnette held numerous Food & Beverage managerial and executive positions with the leader in the gaming and hospitality industry. She was labeled the "go-to gal" within the organization, especially when it came to leading projects that encompassed opening new venues, establishing policies and procedures, orchestrating and facilitating training, and developing future leaders. She was very proud of her identity and worked hard to be the best in the industry, which resulted in her being awarded the prestigious title of "Chairman's Leader of the Year."

While it was a very rewarding career, Larnette felt was something missing. She knew deep in her core that her passion and her purpose were to help people live fulfilled lives, and so she stepped away from the hospitality industry to become a Life Coach. However, leaving a legacy was so important to her that she couldn't shake the identity she'd held for twenty-five years. For the next eight months, this mindset distracted her and stifled her ability to fully engage in her new venture.

But through our work together, we zeroed in on what attributes she could take from her previous identity and which ones to let go of to create a new identity that aligns with who she is now. This process opened the space to see herself exactly how she wants to be seen: as a powerful Life Coach.

YOU CREATE CHAOS

Chaos is a state of complete disorder and confusion. When you have several things going on at once, negative or positive, this can be chaos. Chaos is a multitude of tasks that overwhelm you and tend to take you off your game. Sometimes multitasking can also cause chaos.

You know that life is full of chaos, and some of it is chaos that you choose—created chaos. An example of created chaos is choosing to remodel your kitchen or choosing to take your kids to school in the morning. I think you forget about the chaos you choose, and it's okay to be frustrated because of the chaos sometimes, but it's not okay to ignore what you have created. Step into your chaos and own what you've brought into your life.

Now that you know you've made some of your own chaos, what do you need to own up to, take action on, and change in a healthy way? What chaos do you complain about and how do you plan on stopping it? What happens when you yourself create the chaos? Can you admit that you created it? Can you recognize that you created it? How can you use it for good? Don't be afraid to use chaos for good. You're running around like a chicken with its head cut off anyway—you might as well use it for good.

Of course, sometimes chaos just happens and it's out of your control. This is natural chaos. Some instances of natural chaos might be having a child born with a disease, being the child with the disease, or having a tree fall on your car.

When you are given your chaos, it can be hard to work with because it puts you in a victim mode. You feel like you've been forced to work with it. But you haven't—it's just what you've been given. When it starts to rain, maybe your roof leaks and the smoke detectors go off because your food is burning because you were busy looking at roof, and now the baby has awakened. You didn't create this chaos—it's just life thrown at you all at once. You have all these negative emotions building up with frustration and you don't know what to do. In that moment, you have two choices: you can find the good in the chaos or the bad in that chaos.

When dealing with negative life chaos, people tend to freak out and lose their cool, which is normal. But I'm hoping that after you read this story, you can live happily in your chaos and keep your cool through whatever life throws your way. I highly recommend digging down deep enough to find the good, even if all you uncover is a small sliver of hope and peace. I know this is can be extremely hard to do but finding the good in the chaotic experiences makes life so much easier. And if you can't find the good in chaos, figure out how to make it less painful and minimize your false thoughts around the chaos.

YOUR ATTITUDE TOWARD CHORES

At some point in your life, you chose to see chores as negative. You crafted a new limiting belief that chores suck and don't benefit your well-being. You may feel like someone is forcing you to do your chores.

Are you the type of person who, like me, constantly gets overwhelmed and stressed out when you think about all the chores you have to do? Do you struggle with the workload it takes to keep your life organized, happy, and healthy? Do you work the chores up in your head so that when you get around to doing them, you're already a crazy ball of stress? Does looking at your to-do list give you anxiety? If you answered yes to any of these questions, this section will change your world because chores are a big part of life.

This part of the book is for the people who are sick and tired of being weighed down by something they need, want, and choose to do. Let's be honest—you choose most of your chores. You brought them into your life. Look through all the chores in your life and your unhealthy stories around them. Choose to create a new, healthy story around your chores, and try to love them for what they bring you.

Right now, you see chores as a big horrible time-sucker and life-sucker when they are actually your partners. Chores are a necessity in your lives, helping you stay in balance, happy, and healthy. When you take care of the things you need to take care of for yourself, you feel good and you will finally be on the path toward the right target because you are no longer avoiding your chores. It will feel so good to just do what you say you're going to do and get the chores done with the right attitude.

Create a schedule around your chores that supports you and divide them up among different days if it's right for you. Make sure you set a schedule to protect yourself from burnout and create boundaries that will help you keep that schedule.

Be smart about how you set up your schedule for your chores. Just like when you go to the gym, you want to work a new muscle group every day so that you don't get sore or sick of your routine. Make sure you're always creating new routines and find something fun like music to dance to and distract you from the repetition of chores. Add anything you can think of to make your chores more enjoyable. If you want to change something huge for yourself, make it a priority to maintain a healthy balance in your relationship with your chores. Having fun is so important to creating a happy attitude toward your chores.

People often believe that no one can or will help them with their chores, which makes them feel lonely. When necessary and possible, get help and delegate. Create a team and a schedule of people who can help you. If you have the resources and you're in a family, get everyone to pitch in and help. This is an amazing synergy. Get rid of the isolation and the story around your chores.

There are many stories we make up about our chores. Some people believe chores are useless. try to control their chores and how they are done. And others procrastinate, saying things like "Oh, I can just do that later." There are multiple, different stories that you make up about your chores. What are your stories?

If you are looking for a healthy attitude around your chores, here is a great place to get started. Be aware of where you want to go next, so you can stay on the path to gaining and maintaining a healthy attitude around your chores.

When you are stuck with a terrible negative attitude around your chores, it makes you dread doing them, and you end up hating them, which may make you feel as if you are being forced to do them.

Ask yourself these questions to start relieving the stress, anxiety, and pain around your chores:

- Do you recognize how much power you allow your attitude towards your chores take from you?
- Do you have the attitude of "I have to do it", "I'm all alone", and "No one else can or will help me"?
- Do you isolate yourself in your chores?

The attitude you choose to have with your chores can cause so much internal pain and discomfort. Change your attitude toward your chores today and every day.

A lot Much of the time, making the choices of how you are going to do the chores, when you're going to do them, and how much energy you will give to your chores determines your attitude toward the tasks. You may try to resist your natural ability to take care of all of the things you are responsible for. I don't recommend resenting your chores.

You may feel as though you have no other options around changing your attitude toward your chores. Generally, you do have the option to do it or not, but you choose the option of the negative attitude, saying "I have to" instead of "I get to."

When you choose the path of "I have to," it puts you in the victim state of mind because you gave your power away to the chore itself. There is so much power in choosing your outlook on your chores.

You are blinded by your bad attitude and it creates physical, mental, spiritual, and emotional pain. Most people just tough it out and push through it. You typically have the mindset that if your house isn't spotless, the world is going to end, or if everything isn't perfect for the party, everything is going to blow up.

When you step back, you can start to see that the chore itself is not as problematic as you've made it out to be. You make your chores life or death. You become immersed in the pain of your chores and get stuck with a bad outlook. You tend to resist the truth that it is your choice. I want you to understand that when you have a bad attitude, you tie your hands behind your back. Choose to untie your hands and have a positive and proactive attitude toward getting your chores done. The outcome will allow you to get your chores done faster and more efficiently, and you will be happier, less stressed, and more successful.

I want to be open and share what my chores are, and my attitude change toward them so that you can change *your* attitude. For most, chores mean cleaning the house, mowing the lawn, fixing the car, taking the kids to school, or simply washing the dishes—not life-or-death issues. My chores are different from most other people's chores. For me, my chores consist of calling companies about bills, ordering supplies, getting feeding tube materials, making doctor appointments, and making sure everything comes at the right time. My chores *are* life-or-death—they literally determine whether I live or die.

In doing my chores, the attitude I start with is very important. For the first several years of doing these chores, I had a very self-destructive attitude. My relationship with my chores made me feel like I had a gun to my head and like someone was yelling at me that I had to do it and that I had no choice. Today I have a new, healthy, permanent relationship with my chores. Even though my chores are incredibly difficult to balance, I now work to have a great, relaxed, supportive attitude around them. My poor husband is so grateful that I have a great relationship with my chores.

You're supposed to have a healthy relationship with your chores. Your chores need to get done to support you and to help you be more organized and efficient in your life. They make a huge difference in helping you to be successful. You must create a partnership with your chores to create all the success you desire and deserve in your life.

What chores do you have a bad relationship with? What attitude adjustments do you need to make? For some people, completing chores, no matter how painful, provides peace of mind. How can your chores give you a healthy attitude that creates peace of mind? How can you do your chores pain-free instead of just pushing through them? When you make the choice to do your chores, you can make the choice to do them with an "I want to do it" attitude.

Stand strong in your chores. Love them. Use them. Enjoy the rewards they give you. Look for what the chores bring to your life; You will be amazed by the change, organization, and balance that completed chores give you.

SHIFT YOUR ATTITUDE

It's pretty amazing that you have the ability to change your attitude at any given time. You are very blessed and lucky to have that power over your life. Changing your attitude changes your reality. You know your reality can be changed by a positive attitude or a negative attitude.

What does your day-to-day attitude look like? Do you start the day with a great positive outlook or an attitude that drains your day away? Get curious about why you may have a bad attitude. Where did it come from and what is causing it? If you can find the core of the bad attitude, you can stop it or take the time to work through it. This will help you to keep it from happening and start your day with a great attitude instead.

Sometimes you have a bad attitude for a reason. Be aware of your triggers and the bad attitudes you can get trapped in. You must look at your attitude to relieve it. Do so by giving it the time and attention it needs because you are frustrated or upset about something. You can easily look at it, work through it, and start your day off with the right attitude.

Look, everybody is going to have a bad day every once in a while, but some days you start out with a horrible attitude and you have no clue why. That's okay; it happens to the best of us. If you can't figure out why you have a bad attitude, why let it run your day? You don't even know why you are crabby. The best thing to do with your negative attitude is to simply create a new healthy one. Sometimes you won't know why you're crabby, so just let it go. But if your crankiness comes up over and over again, you will need to look at it and dig deeper.

A negative attitude depletes your happy energy and steals your great moments. I think people forget the importance of their attitude. You don't realize how much power it has over you and your successes. It is crazy that people let their attitude define them and how they're feeling. It's also ridiculous how your attitude creates your reality and you're cool with it. You just go along for the ride. Look into how your attitude creates your reality and see if that's the reality you're truly looking for.

You can use my following script for a quick and easy attitude adjustment. It is a great way to create a permanent, healthy, attitude pattern:

If you want to create your dream attitude for the day and you are in your safe place, close your eyes for a moment. Take three deep breaths and imagine the best attitude you've ever had. Bring in all that good energy and all that brightness from that day. Breathe it all in. Bring in the best emotions and memories, allowing them to fill your entire mind and body with an amazing new attitude. Exhale any stress, tension, anxiety, and frustration that came along with the negative attitude. This is how you can reframe and create the desired attitude. Figure out and connect to what you want to feel and think. Decide in that moment that you will have your desired attitude. Do your best to not allow anything to get in the way of achieving that productive mindset. Choose an attitude that aligns with the day you wish to have.

6

PATTERNS ARE EVERYTHING

HOW ARE YOU CONDITIONED TO MAKE DECISIONS?

You are conditioned in such a way that makes you feel like you are trapped, with no opportunities to make decisions for yourself. You focus so much on the conditions you are trapped in that you forget you have the power to get out of the conditioning patterns. The power to stop conditioning patterns comes from making a great decision and owning it. Give yourself the ability to make a choice and stop the patterns.

A conditioning pattern is when you are trained to do something over and over again, usually unconsciously. A conditioning pattern helps you to feel safe, and you become comfortable in it. It creates a long-term cycle. A conditioning pattern is something that is super hard to stop. It's like you jumped onto a merry-go-round and can't get off.

Can you believe how often you get stuck because you're conditioned to think you have no option to make a decision? It's crazy. Every time you feel trapped ask yourself: am I dependent on the conditioning pattern or am I free to make the choice? Almost always, the answer is that you are free to make the choice, but unconsciously you believe the conditioning pattern is the only way.

You don't always realize it, but you are constantly being conditioned in so many ways. You are conditioned by people such as family, friends, and strangers. You are also conditioned by your environment and anything you come into contact with like social media, television commercials, and Photoshopped magazine images that make people look flawless. Most of the time you go along for the ride. The propaganda leads you to believe this is how it has to be because everybody else is doing it. You're also conditioned to think that because everything is at your fingertips, everything is easy.

Changing your conditioning patterns is nothing like television says it is. Television teaches you that you can have a six-pack in two months if you do x, y, and z. But you know that it takes so much more. Magazines condition you to think that you need to be skinnier and taller and have perfect skin and whiter teeth—that you aren't allowed to look like a normal person. Advertisers know exactly how to get your attention. They know your wants, your desires, your insecurities, and the things you just can't get. They use vivid colors, Photoshop, and attractive people to capture your attention to the point where you can't look away.

But what advertisers do to you, you do to yourself. You get trapped in the emotions of desire and the insecurities that keep you conditioned to do the same thing over and over again. Our society ropes us up like a cowboy ropes cattle. The cattle just get swept off their feet and are oblivious to what's happening. They go along for the ride as though it is normal and no big deal. They are conditioned to have a submissive relationship with the cowboy. I highly recommend that you figure out how television ropes you up and how it makes you feel. I hope you can cowboy up, wrangle your conditioning patterns, and make them submissive to *you* in a healthy way.

An amazing client of mine who works a forecaster was conditioned by her employer to believe that she only got her job because of pure luck. Tyra was told everyday for twelve years that she was not good enough for her job, that she sucked at it, in fact, and that she was too stupid to work anywhere else. They told her they were only keeping her on because it would take too much work to hire and train someone new. They told her she should be grateful to have this job. Basically, they trained her to believe she had to bow down and kiss the bottoms of their shoes, like she was scum on the floor.

My beautiful client became conditioned to think she was scum and couldn't work anywhere else. She thought she was worthless and didn't deserve success or happiness. Tyra was told that it was impossible for her to achieve success and that if she ever were to achieve success, she would not be able to remain successful.

It's astonishing to think that when Tyra came into my practice, she was making twenty thousand dollars a month. She came in saying that she was never going to make it and that there was no way it was going to last. Although she is incredibly successful in her new career, her old employer's conditioning patterns had her thinking that she was nothing without them and that she had no talent. They crushed Tyra's confidence and her ability to be proud of her accomplishments; this took her ten years.

Now that she is aware of how she was conditioned; the real work began: she must create new healthy patterns for herself. She changed by working through each conditioning pattern with hypnotherapy and coaching. She used my multiple scripts, one being the "Voiceless" script and another being "Regain Your True Power." I am grateful to have had the opportunity to coach someone like Tyra to see how beautiful she really is.

The truth set Tyra free. The core of her new patterns is the truth. Her new truth is that she is successful from the inside out. Now that she has worked through her conditioning pattern, she has a new cycle that supports her every day instead of a limiting belief that diminishes her ability to be successful and happy. This amazing client has changed the cycle and changes others' lives every day thanks to freedom from her conditioning patterns. On the verge of making a million dollars a year, she is standing in her power and fighting for herself by creating a new pattern. Tyra has finally reconditioned herself to live her life to the fullest and achieve her greatest dreams.

Once you accept the fact that life is full of pain and hurt, you can begin to eliminate the patterns that control and define you. How often are you conditioned to think the worst or do the worst? Your conditioning patterns are what cause your mind to think in a negative way versus a positive way. When you have given the power to your conditioning patterns, you have allowed the thought process to become ingrained in your mind, and it will play constantly like a broken record until you make a deliberate permanent change.

Now that you know you can choose your conditioning patterns, what do you choose? Do you choose a pattern that controls you, hurts you, or helps you, or will you choose to be stuck where you are? I would take some time to write a list of all the conditioning patterns that you have and that you plan to change. Also, devise a plan for how you will take action. How will you be aware of when new conditioning patterns start, and how will you ensure they are healthy for you? More than anything, how will you condition yourself to know you always have a choice? I hope you choose a pattern that changes your life for the good.

When choosing a new pattern, allow your thoughts to flow in and out of your mind. Decide which ones are going to have power over you and which ones you are going to lean into. If it feels right, allow the thoughts to play out and see what you learn from them. I would like you to look at your conditioning patterns to see how they are serving you and keeping you safe. You have the power to replace old conditioning patterns with beautifully healthy ones, you have the choice to stop your conditioning patterns in the moment, and you have the choice to give in to them or stand up to them.

Standing up to your conditioning patterns takes a lot of courage. Where do you plan to find that courage? You must find the courage to stop your conditioning patterns.

If you really want to overcome your conditioning patterns, start by making a decision to find your inner courage. You may have to look hard and deep, but it's in you. Use your courage to change your conditioned patterns.

INSANITY PATTERNS

There are two types of insanity. One type is a serious mental illness. The other type is doing the same thing over and over again and expecting different results. This is the type of insanity you are probably stuck in, and it's telling you that you can only live within this one pattern, making you feel stuck in your own head. It is natural to get trapped in doing the same things while hoping and expecting something different each time without actually trying something new. This is the game that the insanity patterns play with you. An example of this might be a married couple's having the same argument over and over, never using new tools to get to a different result. This is the most common example I see as a coach. Everybody argues and communicates using the same old tools, and they forget they need more resources. You're so quick to forget that you are not trying anything new, you're trapped, and you are only getting draining energy from the arguments.

If you are trapped in your own insanity pattern and you're ready to get out of your head, you should know it will take hard work to change your thoughts. You have to stop letting insanity control and drive your life, especially when you think a problem can be fixed by doing the same thing over and over. When this happens, you begin feeling overwhelmed and your mind tells you that it's tried everything to stop. In reality, you have only tried what your mind has allowed you to do.

So, what would it take for you to get out of your own head? It's actually much simpler and not as complicated as you make it out to be. In the future, when you get trapped in an insanity pattern, you will already have created and used these tools that I am about to share for yourself to not get trapped. Once you have recognized you are trapped in that insanity pattern, you will instantly be able to put an end to it.

Not only do insanity patterns trap you, but they also hinder your growth. Any time you feel as though you cannot grow, ask yourself, *Am I trapped in an insanity pattern?* I want you to know that it's possible to create something good out of your insanity. Ensure that you don't get trapped in the pattern and instead feel optimistic that there's more that you can do. You just need to think outside the box. Most important, don't give up, because you'll only let yourself down. You can start getting out of your head by being aware that you are, in fact, in your head. With your new awareness, you will need to find new tools and resources to solve this insanity problem. Remember you are not alone. Find a safe, conscious partner to talk to and work through your insanity with. Do some research to solve the problem and use the results as evidence of many other solutions beyond what you have already tried. Also, take the time to recognize that you can't solve the problem the way you have already tried and realize that you have to be willing to get uncomfortable enough to grow out of your insanity patterns.

Genius, Albert Einstein said, "We cannot solve our problems with the same thinking we used when we created them." The biggest steps toward getting out of your head are trusting yourself, having faith, thinking outside the box, and always being aware of your insanity patterns.

7

WHAT HINDERS
YOUR GROWTH

BUILDING BRICK WALLS

You have natural defense mechanisms. The minute you feel threatened or rejected, you start building a brick wall. You generally put up this wall to stop growth, unconsciously or consciously. The wall can extend horizontally for miles, so you can't go around it, and it can extend vertically so that you cannot get over the wall no matter how hard you try. The wall—typically an emotion telling you to protect yourself—keeps you from getting to the other side: something is keeping you blocked, typically an internal or external emotion telling you to protect yourself. Its purpose is to keep people out or to keep yourself in.

It is human nature to instinctively want to protect yourself, but usually you spend so much time *trapped* by these walls. You get so frustrated that it's like you're banging your head on the wall over and over again. Eventually, you get to a point where blood is dripping down your face.

Brick walls are your unhealthy tools to keep others out and your problems in. Essentially, you do this so that you never have to face your problems. You, the wall builder, constantly reinforce the walls, making them thicker, longer, and taller. You are making the walls hard to get over, under, around, or through.

You can be completely unaware that you have put up a wall. It can be hard to face the fact that you have been isolating yourself. It sucks to realize that you have to knock down years and years' worth of walls you have built. It's scary being vulnerable and wall-less when you have had that protection all these years. But at least you get to take it down brick by brick so that you can learn from each piece, healing yourself as you go.

What brick walls have you built that are preventing the growth you so desperately desire? Now that you see those walls, what are you going to do with them? What will it take to demolish your walls?

You were hiding behind your walls, allowing your life to pass you by. For you to effectively take down your wall, you must be ready to be vulnerable and to show up as your true, raw, painful self. The walls take a lot of investigating, strength, time, and energy to demolish. You must be ready to change and grow.

After tearing down the walls, you will need to face conflict in a healthy way and find solutions to your problems instead of just rebuilding the wall. I know you've been hurt, and you are scared, but now is the time to live, not later. Look deep and see what walls you've put up and take them down one brick at a time.

What will it take for you to take action? What will it be like to live a healthy life without walls? When you live without a wall, it is important to set healthy boundaries. Life is easier when you make goals to create healthy boundaries and stick to them. What are you willing to do to live a life without brick walls in your way? If you built the wall, you can take it down. It will require loads of work no excuses and taking action.

Learn from the process of taking your walls down. Remember what they look like so that you may always be free from your walls.

How to Stop Controlling

Controlling is one of those things you know you're doing even though it doesn't serve you, but you do it anyway. I know you have a unique way of controlling different aspects of your life. Sometimes you catch yourself controlling and don't see the harm in it until it becomes a problem. You know there are consequences to controlling your life. One of the biggest consequences you deal with when you try to control your life is that you don't leave room for your Higher Coach to guide you or room for your inner self to guide you to your purpose. You don't let the present moment unfold as the gift it is meant to be.

When people think they are in control of a situation, they think they can prevent any harm from happening to themselves or others. In reality, what they are doing is trying to control every outcome to the point where there isn't room for anything else in the present moment because it's already planned out. Generally speaking, when you plan out everything and it doesn't go how you expected, you experience disappointment because it's not perfect, like you wanted it to be. You are aware that you are trying to control your life. You attempt to plan out everything down to the minute so that you don't get hurt but controlling everything doesn't get you anywhere; It makes you feel alone, hurt, unwanted, and unsure why nothing is working out your way.

What if you stopped controlling everything in your life? There would be room for spontaneity, chances, believing, faith, and connecting with others and your Higher Coach. Since it is highly likely that you will end up disappointed when your plans fall through, why not just be in the moment? You know that moment will never come again.

I want to share a typical account of controlling. This client experience is about a man I'll call Dan. I've been coaching Dan for about six months to help him understand that controlling everything was getting in the way of him living his life. Dan struggled because he thought that if he controlled every aspect of his life he would be able to prevent anything bad from ever happening to him again. He controlled things by forcefully managing everything in his own specific way, making sure it stayed exactly how he wanted it. If he didn't, he would lose it. He felt like he was a failure and his whole life was falling apart.

He couldn't accomplish anything. He thought he wouldn't amount to anything if everything didn't turn out exactly as he planned.

He recognized that he needed to change the way he controls everything so that he could live outside of his head and his own regulations. Before deciding this, he lived a very stressful, anxious, and fear-filled life because he was controlling. Through coaching, he started to slow down enough to breathe again and he got excited about change and the unknown because he knew it would bring him something new and surprising. He also knew that it would be easier to live life with this mindset because he could let go of his stress, anxiety, and worry. Now he is able to enjoy life without controlling, and he says that it is the best gift he has received from coaching yet. He also says that he can't even imagine what his life was like when he controlled everything. He'd been trapped in his own controlling and now he is free.

While answering the following questions, imagine you are talking to me in my role as a coach. These questions are for you to understand your controlling patterns and for you to create an action plan.

1. When and where did you start to use control to work through life?
2. How did it serve you to control your life?
3. When in your life did you feel like you didn't have to be in control?
4. When was the first time you felt good when using control to get what you needed out of life?

5. Why do you think control is the right tool for you to use?

6. Who or what taught you how to control, and how did you turn the process into your own?

7. How old were you the first time you remember controlling things, and how good did it make you feel?

8. How much have you missed out on because of your controlling?

9. When were the times you have tried to control your relationships?

10. What did that control do to your relationships?

11. What power did it give you to control your relationships?

12. How does controlling creep into you home life, your personal life, and your work life?

13. Do you see how controlling hurts you? What you want to do instead?

14. What do you want to get out of your life now that you have the opportunity to be free from controlling?

15. When were the moments in your life that you just sat back, relaxed, and allowed life to happen?

16. How good does it make you feel to be free from controlling?

17. How do you plan to stop controlling everything in your life?

18. What kind of person will you be without your controlling?

19. What choices are you going to make to stop controlling now?

20. Most importantly, are you ready to stand strong and allow life to happen?

You control because it makes you feel safer and it creates the illusion that you have a firm grip on your life. You probably control so that no one can pull a fast one on you, take advantage of you, hurt you, or surprise you. You control because you're terrified to be vulnerable and live in the moment and because you fear the unknown. Of course, there are other reasons, but these are the main ones I have seen as a coach.

I can't wait for you to become control-free. You will realize that control isn't worth losing your life over. When you are free from controlling, you are free to be yourself.

LET GO OF THE IDEA OF BEING PERFECT

Perfectionism stems from a place of wanting to have control. You create certain standards over your life and others' lives and everything else for that matter. Most of the time, it makes others uncomfortable, creates anxiety, and causes the inability to be content. Sometimes the control aspect of being a perfectionist will get you labeled as bossy and someone who can't do anything right for yourself or others. People don't like being bossed around. Because of your high expectations and standards, your connections and relationships suffer tremendously.

I see perfectionism as a gateway drug to your inner critic and your inner pleaser. Perfectionists work relentlessly to please and to make things perfect. Perfectionists believe that once everything is perfect they will be happy, but the truth is that once everything is exactly "perfect," the perfectionist is still not content. They believe that by controlling everything and putting everything in its place, they will know exactly what the outcome will be. They think there is no room for errors. They control, striving for perfection for themselves and everybody else, too. I am sorry to tell you that it just doesn't work like that; the world can't be perfect and neither can you.

Certain personality traits like being obsessively neat, tidy, and meticulous, being dedicatedly on time, and being in command, are key aspects of being a perfectionist, but if you don't get upset when things don't work out exactly as you'd like, you're not a perfectionist per se. This only makes them a perfectionist if they have an unhealthy reaction when things don't work out. Yes, some of those things can be a benefit. However, if you obsess over those things, that's where perfectionism can hurt you and those around you. If you like things neat and tidy but don't get upset when things aren't just the way you want it, then you are not a perfectionist per se. However, if you do freak out in those situations, then now is the time to realize and accept that you are indeed a perfectionist and change this energy because it is hindering you.

Ask yourself, *why do I want to be so perfect?* What does it mean to you? How is perfectionism keeping you safe? What does it give you to demand perfection? Do you recognize how much unhappiness enters your life when you try to be perfect? How does it hinder me and my growth? What is it doing to my relationships and my life? If you expect everything to be perfect, you will be thoroughly disappointed. You might as well live life knowing this now rather than be stuck in the idea that perfection is real. I know you may believe that controlling through perfectionism is the only way to get what you need out of life, but you'll only bring false happiness and heartache on yourself. If you are scared to live without your inner perfectionist, that's okay, but ask yourself if it's really worth living in fear and unhappiness or would it be better to jump in and be free. Be motivated enough to fight for yourself and you will be pleasantly surprised.

What kind of leader are you to yourself if you're asking yourself to be something that doesn't exist? Being perfect isn't your purpose here on Earth. If you always give 110 percent, you'll know that you are doing enough and that you are enough—you don't have to be perfect. Do yourself a favor: let go and allow yourself to go with the flow. Enjoy your messy life—it's fun!

How to Be Beautifully Messy

This is not your typical messiness like a dirty house or a messy car. This isn't the aftermath of a little girl's finger-painting experiment on the walls of the living room or the dirtiness that comes from a one-year-old's first chocolate frosted cake that is covering him from head to toe. In this section of the book, I am not encouraging you to be the type of messy where you live in a pig pen and don't clean up after yourself. I am referring to the messiness of life, the messiness of your own personal emotions, and the messiness of relationships.

Your life is filled with moments of pure imperfection, and that is what makes them beautiful. These moments are raw. The real moments are what give us the gift of messiness because they are unique to us as individuals. It's hard to see how wonderful it is because you are taught that life needs to be perfect even though that's impossible. Messiness, to me, is what life is all about.

The messiness of life and emotions is the messiness you try to avoid and generally try to turn into perfection when you should turn it into purpose. This is the type of messiness you *can't* turn into perfection. This is the unavoidable messiness of your life.

I would like you to think of it in the way that you were not put on this Earth to achieve perfection, nor do I know anyone that is perfect, besides God, of course.

Here are questions to help you better understanding your own messiness and what you want to do with it. Do you even know the messy side of yourself? Do you want to better understand what makes you messy and how it can help you? Have you ever allowed yourself just to be messy? Are you able to accept what you really are—human? Are you the kind of person who avoids messiness?

Do you allow others to be messy around you or do you try to control their messiness, too? What relationships do you need to allow to be messy? What's been holding you back from being messy? Are you afraid that your life and emotions are too hard and messy for others to handle? Do you create the story that your life isn't messy out of fear of judgment?

You can only be you and show people the truth of what you're dealing with. If they don't want to be a part of your messiness, that's their choice. Maybe you need to work on your mess on your own and then come back to the relationship, because sometimes your messiness is just for you to learn from. Don't allow their choice to turn into a judgment on you. Their choice doesn't give you a reason to stop being messy or to stop living your truth.

How can you see more things in life as just messy and beautiful? How can you accept your own messiness? How can you be messier with you family and co-workers? How can you be a leader and show others that it's okay to be their messy selves? Remember not like a pig. What fun memories have you missed out on because you didn't think it was okay to be messy? What goodness in your life has come from your just being messy? What fun and excitement have you had in your life because you allowed yourself to be messy? Don't be afraid to be messy—it's where you'll find a part of yourself you've never met before!

I want you to find the messiness in your life and hold on to it as memories of good, bad, and happy. Start to see your life as a beautiful masterpiece of messiness. See how much easier it is to go through life accepting that life is just messy, yet also wonderfully peaceful and beautiful. We are human and naturally meant to make mistakes and be messy.

Be beautifully you. Be messy. Allow others to be messy. Love your messiness and all the memories that come with it. You are more beautiful as your messy self than you are with the masks of perfection.

BE YOUR OWN COMPETITION

Comparing is the most natural thing you do as a human. You are taught to compare yourself with someone else from the day you come out of the womb. The instant you come into the world, people compare you with your mommy and daddy or even other babies. People may think you have the same eyes, nose, ears, hair, chin, etc. as your parents or relatives. Sometimes even a nurse will compare you with other babies based on look, weight, cry, and so forth. It sounds nearly impossible to stop doing something that's so ingrained, but don't worry—soon you will better understand why it's so important to stop comparing.

You unfairly compare so many parts of yourself with so many other people. We've all had those moments of comparison. For instance, when you go to the grocery store after working on the house all day, you walk in with crazy messy hair, baggy sweats and no makeup. You instantly see someone dressed up and you think to yourself that you should have dressed up more. In that moment, you compared yourself with someone else and probably made yourself feel insecure. Comparing causes tremendous insecurities. I know you understand that feeling from experience and you need nothing further from me to explain it. Comparison feeds your insecurities. So why do it at all?

When you look at what you don't have that others *do* have, you are creating comparative energy, which drains you. It takes the focus off of you. Comparing makes you believe that what you have is not good enough. It tricks you into thinking that what others have is more important than what you have. You should only compare *you* with *you*.

You believe that other people lead perfect lives. When you compare, you believe that everything is perfect for them and that nothing goes wrong for them, as though they are living a perfect life without pain, hurt, mess, mind games, or negative self-talk. How surprising is it that you totally forget about the fact that no one is perfect and everyone has their own set of problems? Think about how much pressure you are putting on your relationships with other people. You are putting them up on a pedestal, which is unfair to both of you. Imagine how good it would feel to be free from holding that other person to a higher standard. They are probably going through just as much crap as you are or possibly something worse.

It never does any good to look at someone else and see what they have and what you don't. I believe God made us all different for a reason. We all have different eye color, height, natural gifts and talents, and personalities. Our differences are all there for a reason: so you can find your path, be beautifully unique, hold your own special place on Earth, and live out your purpose. Comparing allows you to try to be something and someone you're not. The biggest problem with comparing is that it keeps you from looking at yourself and restricts you from being the best you, compared only to you.

I am requesting permission for you to open up a space to be able to play a little game with me. Make sure it is safe for you and then take three deep breaths. I want you to step into a world where the is no such thing as comparing. Can you see how great it feels to have no pressure on yourself and for all the focus to be on yourself? What if you made the choice to only compare you with you? How do you think you would start to feel about yourself? In most cases, you will feel very good. You may also find you need to do a lot of work on yourself to be the best you. It's great to know what you need to do next. Know that this world can be real for you, if you wish and work for it.

Now that you can clearly see the downside of comparing, take action. What kind of self-talk do you think you would start to create if you stopped comparing? Really healthy self-talk. How much do you think you would grow if you just looked at you? My guess would be a lot, because you set the bar high and it's your time to focus on you. How good does it feel to really look at you and see how amazing you are? How cool would it be to have all that extra time and energy to go do something productive in your life? You would definitely find more time, energy, and strength for what you really want to do. Why not make the choice now to stop comparing? Let's make a new permanent healthy mind pattern.

It is a wonderful world when you only compare you with you. Like in a video game, it's even more fun to beat yourself in the game of comparing and level up in your growth and become more successful. Find your path. Be unique. Hold your space on Earth. Live out your purpose to the fullest.

8

FREE YOUR INNER JUDGE

TRUE HAPPINESS THROUGH ACCEPTING OTHERS DESPITE OUR DIFFERENCES

Everybody does something they hate. This one thing in particular is a completely destructive energy. That something that I am referring to is judging. Everybody does it and some people are ashamed that they judge others. People wish that they could get off the autopilot cycle of judging. Here your chance to get off autopilot and free yourself from judging.

Judgers judge themselves and those around them. Often, you get trapped in judgment. You use it to distract yourself from looking at yourself and to make you feel holier than thou. Sometimes, people who judge think there has to be something wrong with others in order for them to feel good about themselves. Other times, people just judge because they are on autopilot or have nothing better to do. Sometimes it's unconscious and isn't driven by meanness or unhealthy energy at all. People are naturally programmed to look at what is wrong with people and judge others for being different. Judgment starts out as natural curiosity and then your mind turns it into something unhealthy. You are such a curious soul—there is nothing wrong with being interested in someone's differences—but it is not up to you to judge them.

Judging consists of completely destructive energy, and life is so much easier if you learn to accept others the way they are. Lack of acceptance makes you and those around you unhappy. The people closest to you are often victims of your non-acceptance and harsh criticism for their failure to meet your expectations. Most people are guided by the mantra "my way or the highway," but that is not an acceptable way to live or think. You have to live your life judgment-free and let others do the same. Think about the reverse; put yourself into someone else's shoes. Would you be happy if people didn't accept you? Would it be okay if they judged you or treated you unfairly? If not, then learn to accept people without judgment. A great way to free yourself from judging is to put yourself in other people's shoes.

ACCEPT YOUR PARTNER WITHOUT JUDGMENT

In a relationship, you often expect your partners to behave in a certain way, and if they don't it becomes a recipe for conflict. There is a misguided judgment that members of a couple must be the same or have to have the same passions, purpose, or emotions. This makes people less tolerant of each other, thereby causing countless divorces and separation. Expecting people to act in a certain way leaves you stressed out and disappointed because they aren't the way you want them to be. You need to accept and embrace others' differences. Otherwise, there is no foundation for the relationship to stand on. What if you just accepted your boyfriend for the reserved, creative, football-loving person he is? Would it change the way he views you? What if you accepted your girlfriend for the talkative, emotional, passionate woman she is? Would it change the way she views you? Would accepting someone make you like them or boost their confidence? Working together is mandatory in any relationship, and experts believe that things are more likely to work out between couples with different personalities glued together by acceptance. I believe that people need a distance between their personalities in order to grow together. People's differences and their unique qualities help them grow together and live inside a new frame of mind, a new perspective. Seeing the other side of what you can't see is very helpful. For example, an extremely emotional person and someone highly logical can create a healthy balance that will help them to solve their relationship problems together with a great balance.

Accepting others is the true mark of unconditional love. Honor yourself and others by respecting, loving, and not judging them. Remember you are human, and people are flawed. Imperfections make people who they are. Focusing on the good in a person helps you realize that you are not perfect and that you are one and the same. Do everything you can to deliberately look for the greatness in the world and its people.

When learning not to judge, avoid making comparisons with others, yourself, and the past. You should remain focused on the present and try to live accordingly. If you judge circumstances or people, it will certainly be difficult to embrace things as they are. Ask yourself why the imperfections you perceive in others bother you. Are they really imperfections in others or shortcomings in yourself? When you identify their shortcomings, reflect on your own and you may realize that at some point in your life, you also have that same judgment of yourself. Once you realize and accept that, you are one with your humility. You will be free of your expectations and judgment of yourself and others.

Humility is when you can put yourself on the same level as others—or lower— into someone else's situation or pain to show them and yourself that you are not judging them, they are not alone, and you've been there. Humility means you are one with whatever is causing you or the other person pain or discomfort. When you make the choice to become one with it, it eliminates the pain and discomfort altogether. It creates good, healthy energy to share. You are able to share similar experiences and relate to each other, and your relationship becomes free of shame, judgment, and embarrassment.

A lot of amazing people judge others. Sometimes you judge others because they do not do what you would do. Let's say you did something nice for someone else and they didn't say thank you. You are probably floored because you find that disrespectful. You yourself always say thank you. You are judging what you think is right or wrong because other people are not like you. They are not meeting your expectations or standards. You don't know how they were raised—all you know is that they don't demonstrate the respect and etiquette that you personally value. Your personal values trigger you to judge. Ask yourself how much of your personal values and expectations you put on others. What personal value is making you trigger to it? Is this supporting or draining your relationships? If it is draining your energy, what are you going to do to change it? How will you create a healthy, permanent pattern? How often do you trigger and judge because of your personal values? How can you be more understanding of others?

HOW TO STOP JUDGING OTHERS AND ACCEPT YOURSELF

Self-acceptance is key to finding true happiness within yourself. You cannot love what you do not accept. There are numerous ways in which you can learn to accept yourself. One way is learning how to be free from judging others. Another way is being conscious of your thoughts. When you practice being mindful of your thoughts, you will be able to recognize when you find yourself in a situation where you are being judgmental. Being mindful of your thoughts is a skill that is important to cultivate in order to stop judging.

Empathy is being able to see and feel what someone else is going through. Empathy is the ability to see things from the other person's perspective and pain. Sometimes you show empathy when you have heard what another person has to say, or you have gone through a similar experience. Sometimes you can just see the pain written all over someone's face and you feel it with them. Many people look at empathy as a character flaw.

They believe empathy is reserved for the weak. The truth of the matter is that it allows you to become a better leader and a more supportive person. Once you accept empathy into your life and heart, you can open up to learning ways to become a person who is mindful of others' thoughts and feelings. Empathy is the best gift to give others. Judgment cannot live in empathy.

Did you know that judging others has an impact on your mood as well as how you feel about yourself? Dig deep and take some time to consider how judgment affects your mood. You may have come across people who put others down unconsciously so that they can feel better about themselves. When you judge a person, you may think you are raising your self-esteem, because in your eyes, you are better than them, but in actuality you are only feeding your false inner critic because judging can never feed you healthy energy. You may feel good about this, but when you dig deep and think about it, you will find that you only feel happy because you have put someone else down to raise yourself up. After you recognize that, you do not feel happy at all. You probably feel frustrated, sad and disappointed in yourself. So, in essence, you are not judging the other person; you are judging yourself. And judging others can never make you truly happy. It can only feed a false fire in yourself that you must extinguish.

9

How to Free Your Inner Pleaser

Know the True Meaning of 'I'm Sorry'

I honestly don't think people use apologies the way they are meant to be used, which as a Life Coach, makes me very sad. It takes a strong person to say, "I'm sorry," and an even stronger person to forgive. It takes a person full of self-worth to say they're sorry only for the right reasons.

A sincere apology should be used when you do something wrong. If you have the opportunity to apologize in the moment when you know that you did something wrong, take it. You will save yourself and others so much heartache if you can sincerely say you're sorry in the moment. However, in this case, you automatically feel remorse and guilt for what you did; the automatic feeling should trigger you to apologize immediately. You are likely making a selfish move by trying to correct the internal/external conflict and pain you have caused, and that is a very natural, human thing to do. But in reality, the apology should be first and foremost about healing the pain you have created for the *other* person; and then you can focus on helping yourself heal. I am proud to say that many of my clients naturally focus on the person they hurt before themselves. I am proud of the people my clients are beneath their pain.

The other huge struggle for people when apologizing is admitting they are wrong. It is the most humbling thing you can do, and people struggle to put their egos and pride aside and say they are wrong right away or at all. But it helps you get through the conflict, and most important, it keeps your ego from having any voice. The best way to apologize is with calm and humility. Your ego cannot survive where those qualities live. There is no shame in saying you are wrong. Setting your pride and ego aside to admit you are wrong is a respectable and attractive thing to do. True leaders know when and how to apologize and admit their faults and defeats. The most important thing to remember is that when you apologize for something, one of the promises you are making is that you won't do it again. You must keep your word or people will never believe you. Although both are powerful, your actions should speak louder than your words.

As for people who constantly apologize for who they are and say, "I'm so sorry," for something they've said or simply for being imperfectly human, that's a very unhealthy way to live life. Are you ready to step into your new power and stop apologizing for who you are? Maybe your sense of humor or vocabulary is different from others' or you are too bubbly for some people—stand up and be who you are. It's important to be respectful and know your audience, but always be your true self and only apologize for things that should be apologized for. Acknowledge if and when you are in the wrong and don't make excuses. Never apologize insincerely; if you can't be sincere, wait to apologize until you can be. Please remember, always man/woman up and apologize when you are truly in the wrong. It's the best way to clear your pain, hurt, and conscience. Surround yourself with those who love and accept you for who you are. Surround yourself with those who will accept your apologies so that you can grow together. You want to be with people who know you're human, understand you're imperfect and will make mistakes, and want you to be the best you.

For most of my life, I said I was sorry for being me. I would go as far as saying I was sorry for the baggage I carried with me—my gifts and abnormalities, my messiness—and for everything I did that was less than perfect. I always felt I had to apologize for my existence. I am here to tell you that this is no way to live your life. It annoyed everyone I had a relationship with; it bugged them to their core because I had nothing to apologize for. It made others feel uncomfortable because they didn't understand why I was apologizing for being me.

I learned this pattern at a very young age, and it was the hardest thing for me to overcome. Because I was a victim of abuse, I had to apologize to keep myself safe. As an adult, after my healing, I feel safe now, because I am; this safety mechanism is no longer necessary, but back then I put it in place for survival.

Once you are thriving in life, you will see that the "I'm sorry" will no longer serve you. If you are on autopilot in apologizing, say this every day or as often as possible: "I am free from apologizing for no reason. I will only apologize in a healthy way."

So how about stepping back to see if your apologies are on autopilot or are coming straight from your heart? Do your actions truly deserve an apology? The more you apologize the less of an impact it will carry. So, figure out if it is completely warranted. Do yourself and those around you the biggest favor: change the way you apologize. Please, stop unnecessary apologies and save them for when you truly mean it and need it. If you always acknowledge and apologize when you are in the wrong, your life and your relationships will reap the benefits.

HOW TO STOP PEOPLE-PLEASING

People-pleasing happens for several reasons. Sometimes it's ingrained in you from childhood. Other times it can happen when you feel a strong desire for approval or love or because you simply want to avoid conflict. Often, you would much rather be a savior to avoid looking within because it is easier than facing your feelings of selfishness, guilt or obligation. Most people get trapped in people-pleasing because it helps them feel less lonely, more important, and most of all needed, even if it's unhealthy.

Everyone starts out with a need to be safe, loved, and accepted. It's in your DNA. Many people believe that the best way to do this is to put aside what they want or feel and allow someone else's needs and feelings to take precedence.

This works for a while—it feels natural and there's less outer conflict—but the consequence is that your internal conflict continues to grow. If you decide to say no, you feel guilty, and when you say yes, you may feel resentful toward the other person. You're darned if you do and darned if you don't.

A people-pleaser is one of the nicest and most helpful people you'll ever have the pleasure of knowing. They never say no, and you can always count on them for a favor. In fact, they spend a great deal of time doing things for other people, which makes them think they are fulfilled when in reality they aren't. People-pleasers can become overwhelming or annoying because of their need to seek approval from you, though they are good people and mean well. They always do what's best for others but rarely think about what's best for themselves. Obviously over time, permanent burnout occurs, physically, emotionally, and spiritually. You will end up feeding off the people-pleasing energy and will come to rely on it. This is an unhealthy way to live and an unhealthy way to receive love. Being in any relationship with a people-pleaser is uncomfortable because in some way or another, they will either be resentful toward you or feel rejected by you; there will be some unknown conflict you will have to face.

The underlying cause of being a people-pleaser may be fear-based: you may believe you will not be loved if you do not aim to please. If you don't receive others' approval, you feel as though your whole world will shatter and fall to pieces.

Being in an intimate partnership with a people-pleaser may cause a relationship to suffer. People-pleasers give and give to their partner but feel unappreciated or unimportant and that their needs and desires aren't considered. It is difficult for a people-pleaser to understand why their partner won't give as much in return. It doesn't make any sense; in fact, it frustrates a people-pleaser beyond belief. They feel taken advantage of and walked over, like a doormat. Make today the day that you stop people-pleasing, please. Save yourself and your relationship.

Your mind only knows that "if I give up being a people pleaser, I have to deal with fear." It is afraid of disapproval, and it would rather be in discomfort than lose the false feeling of unconditional love and acceptance. People-pleasers can limit themselves to three choices: pleasure, pain, or fear. They'd much rather live their life in the insanity of the pattern they have created for themselves than face the negative, sometimes at any cost.

JESSICA'S INNER PLEASER

Here's a client story about Jessica's desperate need for love and acceptance. As a kid, Jessica was not at all popular. In fact, she had secured a position for herself in the "uncool" kid category. Thank God there were other "uncool" kids like her who became her friends. Sadly, this did not last forever. In the first year of junior high school, those friends abandoned her. They joined the cooler group, and she still was in the same "uncool" position. Only now she was alone, with no one to depend on. She tried anything and everything to please others and gain their friendship and affections. They broke her heart. She was triggered into believing that the only thing she could do was people-please.

She became an introvert. People commented on how shy and skinny she was and how tired she looked. This made her aware of the two important categories: ugly, where people didn't like her, and good-looking, where everyone did. She switched from a private school to a public school to start life fresh, hoping to find new friends to like her. Tired of all the negative comments she received, she started taking care of herself and began using makeup. And this did change things—it gave her confidence. She pleased society and her peers by playing dress-up and pretending to be someone everyone else wanted her to be. People started noticing her. They became her friends, and even love interests started pouring in. All she knew was that she was getting noticed but she wasn't being herself. Being a tomboy, Jessica didn't like all the makeup and girlie stuff. She was doing all of this for approval and to please others, so she would fit in.

She loved this for a while but gradually started realizing how meaningless all the fakeness was. Even though people would say appearance is not all that important, they would still categorize and judge others as either good-looking or ugly. What was underneath her skin was not important to others; how she looked was all that mattered. However, inside she knew that there was much more to her than just her girlie looks.

She came to the realization during her coaching sessions with me that the way she was approaching her life was holding her back. She believed love meant working for others' approval and being what they wanted her to be. She didn't think she was allowed to be who she really wanted to be, the quirky one. She needed to relearn how to be her true self and how to stop people-pleasing for love and friendship. She needed to have faith that who she truly is -- is enough. Yes, she needed love, but she now wanted to be loved for who she was *inside*. She wanted to be able to love herself again, too. She made a choice to be who she is and share herself with the world.

Her first step was to start being herself with everyone she could. She had to trust that if they were truly her friend, they would remain her friend. If not, she loved herself enough to know that the loss of a friendship was less important than the loss of herself.

EVELYN

This client has been a people-pleaser since she was a little girl because it was how she was raised. People-pleasing was ingrained in her, and it became a permanent pattern. She aimed to please everyone, including her husband, children, and neighbors. She could never say no to anyone or anything.

Doing things for herself was a luxury that she considered selfish. She waited till her late forties to get her first pedicure because it was a luxury! She would never simply order pizza for dinner because she believed it would make her look lazy; her limiting belief system was that the only way to please her husband was to make a homemade dinner.

She was always so busy doing for others, and as time went by, she became more and more exhausted and burned out because she was trying to do it all by herself. She felt so unappreciated, especially by her husband. She ended up divorced but went right back into another relationship where she couldn't say no. She was so worried about hurting other people's feelings that she became exceedingly drained physically and emotionally all over again.

She tried to ask for what she wanted but never got it, so she continued to people-please to keep the peace. She was trapped in her own patterns and had to stop and figure out what she wanted to do. She had to decide what was on her list of priorities and needs for herself, even though it was scary, new, and uncomfortable. She had to face the fact that she couldn't care if they liked her, needed her, or wanted her around. She had to stop pleasing for love, safety, and acceptance. When she stopped pleasing, she found out who her true friends were, which was hard for her. They weren't who she'd expected. She tried to please others for so long by following their values, beliefs, and ethics to please-people that she forgot she had values and ethics of her own that meant the world to her. It was very difficult to stand up for her beliefs, but in the long run she is happier. She also had to accept that certain things were not luxuries or selfish. She realized that when she made more time for herself, she was a better person, less exhausted and actually had more quality time for others.

This newfound compassion for herself is much healthier for her. She says she will never go back to her old ways, because she now knows life is so much better when she is not trying to please others.

LEARNING TO LOVE YOURSELF AND QUIT PEOPLE-PLEASING

As a pleaser, you want to do everything you can to impress others. What happens is when people appreciate you, you feel good about yourself. The downfall is when they take you for granted, you feel horrible; sometimes this leads you to believe that you are not worthy of their love. Be aware if your appreciation value is triggered on top of your inner people pleaser.

Everybody wants to be loved, to enjoy the feeling that you are important or special to someone, and to have the feeling of a loved one needing us. Those feelings can be healthy, meaningful, and beautiful. This is healthy love that cannot be obtained through people-pleasing; this is real love. If someone truly loves you, it won't be skin-deep—it will be for who you are.

Then there is unhealthy love. The type of love that you receive from people-pleasing, that only gets in the way of experiencing true love that reaches your soul and heart. Being a people-pleaser gives you the temporary feeling that you are liked and loved and falsely fulfills you. When you are being falsely fulfilled, you don't feel "selfish" because you aren't giving any love to yourself. Instead, you're giving it away to everybody else.

Loving yourself will help you let go of being a people-pleaser. When you are learning to step into your power, it can be hard to love yourself, because you are so used to feeding off of unhealthy love. You probably have no clue where to start, but that's okay. You only have to answer one question right now: are you ready to be free from pleasing and meet your own needs? Putting time and energy into loving yourself is a great step toward quitting people-pleasing, it is comparable to quitting a bad habit. Because it was an automatic pattern, you may experience some form of withdrawal. The best way to get through such withdrawal is through self-love, awareness, and staying consistent with your new pattern. After quitting, you will realize your energy is sustainable, constant, reliable, and beneficial because you will have gained confidence and strength.

It's important to accept that not everyone will like you. You do not like everyone, so if everyone does not like you, that is perfectly normal. To begin the process of quitting being a people pleaser and starting to love yourself, write down five to ten things you like about yourself. What do you like? What do you love? What makes you who you are? What makes you unique and special? If you can't think of anything to write, start creating things in your life that you love and things that make you happy. There are no excuses when you are letting go of your inner people-pleaser.

Read your list daily and add to it as often as possible. You have to find your inner good—that's your job. Only then will you start to please yourself and have healthier relationships with the people you care about. The less you seek approval the more your inner love and inner strength will grow. You will no longer feel a need to please. You will just be in a healthy state of mind, ready to enjoy life knowing that you don't have to please to receive love.

What fuels your people-pleaser the most is thinking that all you *are* is a people-pleaser. Your pleaser causes you to become defensive; you think you can't let go of protecting your character. But you are more than a people-pleaser. You do not have to be a pleaser to be a good person. How much happier would you be if you did things without aiming to please others?

What do you think your life would look like if you were free from this energy and these patterns? There is so much more to you for people to love than your desire to please.

I know it is scary living with your inner pleaser. I know it is hard to live without a piece of you. But you will be so much happier when you are able to love yourself for who you are without your inner pleaser.

LEARN TO SAY A FIRM NO

When you make excuses for saying no, it is normally because you don't want to hurt anyone's feelings, and that opens the door to negotiations. That is when your inner pleaser creeps up, making you do what you really want to say no to. You need to learn to say a firm "no" and be truthful or you will continue to be the victim of your own decisions. Saying no to pressure is hard, but that's what life is all about, not leaning into the temptation or the pressure.

No is a word that people pleasers rarely if ever say. It's a word that leads to the feeling of letting someone down, which then leads you to feel as though you are unkind and even selfish or unworthy. People-pleasers feel guilty if they say no.

Even if you want to say no, with just a little pressure from your inner pleaser and the person wanting something from you, you will probably cave in and say yes. In the instances when you have said no, you came up with so many reasons to justify why you said no and as many reasons why you should have said yes. You probably feel guilt for refusing to please someone but know that you do not need to be at the beck and call of everyone else to receive love, be kind, and feel worthy.

Because you said yes when you wanted to say no, you now have to face the many consequences and *own* the fact that you yourself created unhappiness. The reality is, you will probably take your decision to say yes out on the other person in some way. You become the victim of your inner pleaser's choice, and the "yes" decision you made was rooted in negative energy because you intended to say no. However, because you didn't, it could ultimately end up in failure and possibly resentment. All of this is because you did not want to hurt the other person's feelings. Usually this makes the whole situation blow up in your face, hurting both parties involved.

The best advice I can give you for avoiding all this unhealthy behavior is to say no when you want to say no. You and the other person deserve more. Don't forget that the person has no idea that you are people-pleasing and may believe you are being genuine. Learn to say no and to say yes to making your own decisions. You can do this because you are strong enough to take charge of your own life.

BE THE LEADER YOU WISH TO SEE IN THE WORLD

Trust that your initial decision to say no is the right thing. Follow your instincts. By doing so, you will ultimately be a better leader with more supportive energy because you have not taken on the stress of putting everyone else's needs before your own. Instead, you will take care of your needs while simultaneously leading others to independently take care of their own needs. A healthy "yes" or "no" does not need a justification, because it is truly what you want and what's best for you. A true leader shares their wants and needs with others.

There are different situations that people-pleasers get trapped in. Sometimes they put themselves there and unconsciously allow themselves to be walked all over. However, a true leader knows a healthy way to respond. Here are examples of unhealthy and healthy responses:

Jack's Unhealthy Answer:

Jane: Could you come over tonight and help me set up my new TV?

Jack: I really don't feel well. Could we do it another night?

Jane: Oh, but, Jack, I really want to watch TV tonight. You're the only one I can count on

Jack: Well, I guess I can push through it instead of resting. I'll be there in a few minutes, but I can't stay long.

Jane: Oh, thank you so much. You're so great! I just need a couple hours of your time.

Jack: Okay. I'll be there soon. Hopefully I'll feel better when I get there.

Jack's Healthy Answer:

Jane: Could you come over tonight and help me set up my new TV?

Jack: No, I'm too sick tonight. I have to rest.

Jane: But, Jack, I really wanted to watch TV tonight. I'm so lonely. I have nothing to do. If you don't set it up tonight, I'll be left with nothing.

Jack: My answer is "no," but I would love to help you find a solution.

(When you get to this point, it is up to you. You can just say no, offer other solutions, or explanations, only do if you are not trying to people please.)

Jane: Okay, well, thanks anyway. I'll see if I can find someone else because I really don't know how to do it myself.

Jack: Okay, well, I'm looking forward to seeing how it works out.

Jane: Rest well, Jack. Bye.

In the unhealthy example, Jack was sick and really didn't want to go to her house. In the first scenario, Jane played the victim. Out of guilt, habit, obligation and feeling sorry for her, Jack decided to go help her. But he needed the rest and needed to give her a firm "no." He became the victim of his decision. When he got to Jane's house, he was angry, tired, and frustrated; he was already feeling resentment. He tried to hide it but was unsuccessful. Jane could tell he didn't want to be there, which ruined all the fun of getting a new TV. Jack thought to himself, *this is so disrespectful. I can't believe she asked me to come over right now.* It caused hard feelings and put a strain on their relationship. All this because Jack decided to please Jane, didn't say no, and didn't put his own needs first like he should have.

In trying to convince Jack's inner people-pleaser to set up the TV, Jane said, "If you don't set it up tonight, I'll be left with nothing." Instead, she might also have said things such as:

- "You are so selfish."
- "It would be a nice gesture if you could help me."
- "I could really use your help."
- "I can't do it alone."
- "I thought you loved me."
- "My world would be shattered without you."

As a leader and not a people-pleaser, it is up to you to recognize and deflect these kinds of convincing phrases when people won't take your original "no" for an answer. You have to stand up for yourself so that you are not seen as a doormat to be walked all over. People will learn to respect you if you do. I recommend adding more phrases to the list above from your own personal experience so you can easily spot them when they come up. If you have a written list, it will help you to stay aware of the difference between people-pleasing and real life. Your inner people-pleaser is relentless, so it is important to keep this list to remind you how to not be a people pleaser, to say a firm no, and to be a leader.

In the healthy example, Jack confidently refused going to Jane's to help with the TV. From the get-go, Jack gave her a healthy "no," which allowed him to take leadership of his needs.

He could not and would not put his health in jeopardy. Jane still tried to pull out the victim card, but Jack didn't give into her. Because of the leader that he is, Jack set a boundary with Jane, which then helped the conversation end with no hard feelings or strain on the relationship. Without people-pleasing, Jack did help Jane find other solutions to her problem.

Where are you going to start saying no and standing your ground? A real leader knows when to say no. A real leader leads others to make healthy decisions for themselves. How are you going to be the leader you wish you see in the world?

SET BOUNDARIES WITH YOUR PLEASER

A necessity for getting rid of a people-pleaser is setting boundaries. To begin, find a quiet place and take some good, healthy, deep breaths. Use this time to release anything that is not related to your people-pleasing energy. Hone in on the people-pleaser energy. This will encourage breakthroughs.

Now write down answers to the following questions:

- What was the most recent thing you did that you really didn't want to do?
- Why did you decide to say yes?
- How did you feel when you did it?
- How did you feel about the outcome?
- How you will create a new boundary without people-pleasing, and what will it take?
- What is your action plan?
- How will you say a healthy "yes" without your inner people-pleaser?

- How will you say a healthy, confident "yes" to your new boundaries without excuses? (This will ensure that any future boundaries will be set in stone and not be crossed.)

You can repeat these steps if you wish to create more than one boundary. Use the pain from your pleaser and your experiences to help you become a better person and you will be on the right path to healthy boundaries and freedom from your pleaser.

Learn from these decisions and turn them into opportunities.

Take action with your boundaries! Enjoy being without your pleaser. When you are permanently free from pleasing, throw yourself a party. You should celebrate the outcome, good or bad, embracing the moment. First with yourself, then with your support system—just a conversation with someone else in which you share your gratitude for following through with the win-win decision of finding freedom from being a people-pleaser.

Woot-woot! Celebrate your hard work and keep going. There is always more growth to achieve.

10

HOW SELF-TALK AFFECTS OUR MINDSET

HOW TO CREATE RESPECTFUL, SUPPORTIVE SELF-TALK

You probably wish your self-talk were as kind, caring, and sweet as you are toward everyone else. When it comes to self-talk, you should treat yourself the way you think everybody should be treated, only better. You can cause more damage to yourself than anyone else ever can. No matter how great your self-talk already is, it can always get better. Beware of how you talk to yourself, because you are listening and believing every single word.

Self-talk is how you talk to yourself or how you talk to others about yourself, both internally and externally and usually negatively. You plant seeds about yourself and turn them into a story that plays over and over in your mind, like a broken record. Self-talk is one of the things you give all your power to. Your internal dialogue negatively progresses each day, breaking you down one thought at a time.

If you have healthy self-talk, you can do anything you put your mind to because your communication with yourself is on point, productive, respectful, kind, and encouraging. Let's be honest, most people aren't there yet. People don't utilize self-talk for its true purpose. I believe self-talk is there to encourage you, to support you, and, most important, to help you speak to yourself with respect, honor, humility, kindness and dignity. I also believe your self-talk is your healthy partner in crime; it is there to help you work through your life. Your mind is trained to go straight to the negative. Knowing that, it makes sense that people think it's impossible to move up in the world. It also makes sense that people are always self-sabotaging when it comes to their self-talk. This happens because they aren't aware of their inner chatter. They just allow their mind to talk and talk and talk, filling their mind, body, and soul with toxic draining patterns of negative inner dialogue. This will continue until they get so sick and tired of it that they awaken to the pain and the insanity of negative self-talk.

If you're ready to stop hurting yourself with your inner communication, stop using negative phrases and replace the negativity with supportive self-talk. You can always replace your self-talk with the truth; most of the time, you use your self-talk to lie to yourself. Let's say you have a good set of rolls on your stomach. You may tell yourself that your fat; the truth may be that you're not in perfect health and you may not love how your body looks. Why is that necessary to call yourself a fat cow? Instead, your self-talk should sound like something more along the lines of "I am overweight, and I am not as healthy as I want to be. Today is the day I take action on being healthier." Why do you have to be so mean, so degrading to yourself? The thing about self-talk is that if you don't follow through, your mind will start believing that it isn't possible for you to achieve your goal and you will go back to the old patterns of calling yourself a fat cow. No one wants that—except your inner critic.

Be nice to yourself. Take action on the things about yourself that you don't love and learn the benefit of having supportive self-talk. If you aren't willing to change something about yourself, what's the point of being a nag on yourself? Own who you are! I know it can be hard to be nice to yourself, but why bring more struggles to your life when there is so much negativity in the world already? Why would you want to create another bully in the world when the world is already filled with them? How could a singer go on stage and blow people away with a beautiful song in a brave and powerful way if she talks to herself with disrespect and puts herself down?

Here are some questions to help you start the process of being nice and respectful to yourself:

1. How do you talk to yourself when no one is listening?
2. If other people could hear you, what would you be embarrassed by and what would you have to change? Always talk to yourself as though other people can

hear. This will provide you with a new perspective on how you should talk to yourself.

3. How do you talk about yourself out loud in front of others? In most cases it's not in a confident, loving way.

4. Sometimes your inner critic gets in the way and gives you false confidence. How does your inner critic drive your false confidence? How do you let your inner critic control your self-talk and how you talk out loud?

5. How do you talk to yourself when you are at work? At home? In a healthy or unhealthy way? What actions do you need to take to change your self-talk?

6. What does your negative self-talk do to your communication with others?

7. What self-sabotaging thoughts do you have with yourself and with your relationships? Now that you know what they are, how are you going to change them?

8. How much time have you spent working on creating healthy self-talk for your yourself? I encourage you to make this a priority. Self-talk is vital to your growth. To be the best leader in the world, you must have healthy self-talk.

9. What will it take for you to give your true leader healthy self-talk?

Take your power back. Change the way you talk to and about yourself. In doing so, you will grow immensely. Most important, you will be free of one of your inner bullies. All you have to do is make a choice to talk to yourself differently and supportively. What really hinders your growth is what you whisper to yourself and the overall power you give your self-talk. Maintaining healthy self-talk requires you to always be conscious of what you are saying and think about yourself.

Ego Versus Inner Confidence

Everybody has an ego. What varies is how we let it control and drive us. You are unconscious of your ego and its powers over you. To see your ego, you need to acknowledge that it has its own unique attitude, identity, and inner voice that questions you. Your ego keeps you as its victim. Many people feel as if they have been prisoner to their egos throughout their lives because it has magical powers to control them. It drives people to a point of no return.

Ego can only be in the past or the future, not in the present. Because it cannot exist in the present moment, ego cannot stand in moments of silence, calmness, happiness, joy, peace, confidence, success, or freedom. When you're in the present, watch for signs that your ego is trying to steal your calmness. Your ego needs you to worry and feel fearful in order for it to survive. Beware—it sneaks up on you when it gets bored, which is when you're happy. Your ego creates chaos, distractions, and mayhem. It's a little devil child.

It doesn't like to be told what to do or that it's wrong or be questioned. Your ego can't do anything good; it gives you false confidence and blinds you to the truth. Your ego loves to play off your fantasies, your need to be seen as "the best," your need to be validated, your insecurities and what you don't have. It destroys your belief systems and creates a new one of its own for its own benefit, and it manipulates you into thinking it is the only thing that can help you and keep you safe.

Your ego doesn't allow you to see the true you. Without your ego, you feel powerless, rejected, and weak. It grabs your biggest fears, feeds you as you feed it and turns your worst nightmares into reality. Sometimes your ego will do this for several years, sometimes for decades, and other times for a lifetime. It tells you that you need to know everything to feel in control.

Being egocentric means you think you are the best of the best, no one can beat you, no one knows more than you, you're perfect, you don't need to change or work through anything, you believe that you can walk on water, and your poop doesn't stink. Of course, there is a story your ego tells you. It is the story that manipulates you and teaches you that you cannot survive without it. The story tells you that the only reason you are successful or safe is because of your ego. You are controlling everything in your life to avoid the unknown, and that is exactly where your ego wants you. It will push you hard to know something, to prove you're right, even if it means pushing both parties over the edge. Your ego rarely has proof.

A helpful way to identify ego is to make a list to show yourself how draining your ego is. You need to think about and acknowledge all the times you have pushed to win an argument because you "knew" you were right even though you didn't have all the facts to back yourself up. Later you questioned why you felt the need to fight so hard to be right. You may even have begun to feel like it wasn't as big a deal as you'd made it out to be because you didn't have an attachment to the argument you were making anymore. This list will help you identify the changes that need to be made for the sake of the present and future choices you need to make.

Now can you see your ego? It's important to recognize how your ego has made decisions for you and how damaging it has been to your life. What does your ego look like? Now that you've learned about some of the sabotaging that's happened, do you want to eliminate its control? The best way to eliminate the hold it has on you is to stay present. Your ego cannot exist if you have given up the need to control the next thing that is coming.

Now that you've made the decision to cut ties with your ego, you can start to connect with yourself. You can start to feel the difference between your ego and inner confidence. Life will be so much better once you have found your inner confidence. Your inner confidence loves calm, which is how you identify the difference between your inner-confidence and your ego. Your inner confidence appreciates the silence and allows you to have a minute to breathe, to stand still and decide in the moment without interruption. Inner confidence doesn't have to be right. It trusts, it knows how to handle your life situations and it isn't scared of anything. Your inner confidence uses your pain for fuel to stand up to your ego. It is strong and beautiful. Finally, your inner confidence empowers you to stop second-guessing yourself and grow into who you were destined to be. It's hard work fighting your ego, but it's worth it.

A tool to separate your ego and your inner confidence is to find the truth inside your confident voice. You can feel this choice in your gut. It feels amazing; it keeps you focused, feels right, and is calming, passionate, and purposeful. Grab on to all those good feelings so that the next time you get into a conversation, you will know the difference between your ego and your inner confidence. Listen to your confident voice, trust it, hear it, and feel it. It will lead you in the right direction.

11

FIND SELF-WORTH INSIDE YOUR INSECURITY

LETTING GO OF YOUR JEALOUSY TAKES HARD WORK

Jealousy is that feeling when you are insecure and are afraid of not being enough. Just about anything can spark envy: people, belongings, life situations, successes, and emotions. You can be jealous because you think someone had it easier than you, and you believe that they were handed an opportunity you were not given. Jealousy can occur when you want what other people have. It is a really dirty energy, and no one feels good when they are jealous. Jealousy is an energy that most people are ashamed of. People would do anything to avoid working on their jealousy problems. I don't blame them. No one wants to admit they are envious, but the minute you do, half the battle of breaking the jealousy cycle is won. The other half must be worked through with patience, care, understanding, dedication, and hard work. It also takes sitting in your humiliation with your jealousy and working through it.

Let's talk about where jealousy comes up the most: in your relationships. Many of my clients are jealous because they don't trust the people they have relationships with. They are jealous because of their unconscious insecurities. Between lack of trust and multiple insecurities, I don't know how any relationship is supposed to be successful.

Because of jealousy, you have a need to be in control. You control the situation so that the other person, as well as yourself, will believe they are safe from making a mistake or doing something that causes you to be jealous. As you know, the more you control something the worse it gets. In this instance, the more you control the more your insecurity patterns and your lack of trust are fed.

What is your action plan to figure out how jealousy is seeping into your relationships? What is your plan to stop your jealousy patterns, and what healthy thought processes will you replace it with? If someone is jealous of their brother, they could choose to be happy that he is getting love and attention instead of sulking about the fact that they are not receiving as much. They replace the jealous thoughts with the belief that they are happy that their brother is getting the love and attention he needs. This also helps them to stop taking things personally, and when they think about someone else's needs it eliminates the jealousy because they know their brother needs the love and attention, too. There are all sorts of way to let go of your jealousy; this is just one example. Take the opportunity to find your way!

Now let's talk about how your jealousy feeds your ego and inner critic. You long to be the best of the best, and this is where you get into trouble because—you want to be better than someone else and receive all the recognition and the safety that come with being the best. If you are the best of the best, your ego tells you that you are safe from being left behind. This is how your ego tells you stories. It feeds your jealousy, which in turn feeds your inner critic. It tells you that if you're the best of the best, there will be no need to be jealous, because there will be no one better than you to be jealous of. Your ego and your jealousy work hand in hand to create unhealthy comparing and competitive energy, and you end up with resentment and more baggage to lug along. Your ego, your inner critic, and your jealousy are a ragtag gang that works together to create problems for you and everyone around you. They conspire against you, and it is your job to stop feeding them and change for the better.

Jealousy can lead to so many horrendous things. It never serves you. Being jealous is an energy that makes you feel nasty, resentful, and as if you are lacking. Why be jealous? This is the first question to ask yourself the instant you feel envious. Your answer may tell you whether you are ready to simply let it go, or it may tell you why you're feeling the way you are. Use this answer to help you eliminate your jealous emotions and energy. Get to the core of your jealousy. I want you to ask yourself how does jealousy support you or hurts you? How does it make you feel when you're jealous? Has jealousy destroyed your relationships or your job opportunities? If so, how will you make a plan and take action to stop your old jealousy patterns? How is jealousy distracting you from facing your problems? What insecurities do you have that are causing you to be jealous? How long have you been jealous? Jealousy doesn't look beautiful on anybody. Do everything you can to free the emotions and pain that come with being jealous so that you can be beautifully messy again.

Jealousy is an insecurity. Many jealousy issues arise because you don't trust. Maybe you've been cheated on, abandoned, not treated equally, or respectfully. Maybe you don't have the things others have. Maybe it's time for you to start trusting again and see what happens to your jealousy.

Jealousy has many faces. Go into your past and present life and identify why you are using this tool to serve you when it is just destroying relationships and opportunities. How do you justify your jealousy? Tell me what would happen if you chose to work through your relationships without jealousy. What emotional mind frame would you choose instead of jealousy? Centeredness? Supportiveness? Trust? The best way to be free from jealousy is to be free from insecurity. Please don't be ashamed of your jealousy. Instead, use it to fuel you to create and live a life without it.

HOW TO SEE YOUR INSECURITIES AND TURN THEM INTO SELF-WORTH

Wow! Aren't we humans great at hiding our personal insecurities, what they mean to us, and how they make us feel? You generally play out your insecurities in many different ways and not just by yourself but in front of others. People will go to the ends of the Earth to hide their secrets, their insecurities.

There are different types of insecurities that need to be identified so you can see them and the various roles they play in your life. Here are some examples of some of the insecurities that I see in my practice. It is important to recognize that everybody's insecurities are different. Some people have insecurities about their body image, whether it be that they don't have enough, or they have too much. This may include not feeling pretty enough. Intelligence insecurities, feeling like they're too much of a know-it-all or not smart enough. Some have emotional insecurities such as being too sensitive and crying all the time or lacking compassion and not showing any emotions at all. Some even have insecurities about being insecure. These are just a few of the many types of insecurities. What insecurities do you have?

One of my past insecurities that I had to let go of was my belief that I talked too much. The truth is, I am who I am. I do talk a lot, but that's my personality, my form of communication, how I share my life and love with others, and it is part of my job to speak a lot.

Your insecurities are fueled by being hidden and allowed to play out unconsciously. I believe that if you would just share your insecurities with supportive, safe, nonjudgmental people in your life, it would ease the insecurities and help you understand the truth about your them and yourself. If you don't have that option, I recommend you hire a listening ear to help you through this. You may think that everybody else is confident and that they don't have their own insecurities, but I have never met someone who didn't have some type of insecurity. How sad is it that everybody is walking around with this deep pain and the burden of hiding it? My main purpose in writing this section is to help people to let go of the heaviness of their painful insecurities. No one deserves to walk around this beautiful planet with such deep wounds. Are you ready to dive into your insecurities?

Insecurities are a place where you can get to the power of your worth. You must first be willing to make the choice to let go of your insecurities. The most common insecurity I hear about is the belief that someone's partner is cheating on them, usually with no proof at all, except for the stories they work up in their minds. People become insecure and start thinking they are not enough. By letting the insecurity take over, they allow it to drive a wedge in their relationship and the trust between you and your partner. Sometimes insecurities are created from the breaking of trust in a past relationship and we allow it to affect our current trust, future relationships and our overall happiness.

To be frank, if you can't build trust and you can't find worth in yourself or the relationship, you have no business being in the relationship. If that is the case, you are in a toxic relationship full of insecurities. You need to either choose to trust or let go of the relationship. If they have cheated or broken your trust and you choose to stay, you must also choose to trust. Otherwise, what's the point of the relationship? More than anything, you're fueling the insanity pattern that is feeding your insecurities, leaving you empty, insecure, alone, and isolated, which is exactly what your inner critic wants you to be. Make today the day you break this awful pattern. To find self-worth, you have to build trust.

One way to break insecurities is to just trust and have the faith that you will overcome it. Everyone has had someone break their trust. Personally, I would rather take the risk of trusting over and over than allow the insecurity to overpower me. I know that the consequence could be the person might not deserve my trust, but it's more important to stand in a place where you trust, because it doesn't change your self-worth. It hurts when you give someone the gift of your trust and they break it, but I believe that it is so much more important to keep my self-worth than to play the game of insecurities. It is very hard to keep your self-worth protected from your insecurities, especially when your insecurities are trying to control and diminish you.

Take a moment to take a few deep breaths and see what it would look like if you let your worth lead you through life. To be able to let your worth drive your life, you have to let your insecurities go. To do *that*, you have to identify the deep connection you have with your insecurities. You must shine a light on them and destroy them. You also have to debunk them. You have to do the difficult work of changing the patterns. This will allow the goodness of your worth to shine through and you will be able to believe you're worthy.

Once you're willing to tell your insecurity to talk to the hand, you will regain your self-worth or find it for the first time. You should be excited to build up your self-worth. Seeing yourself as worthy is priceless and achievable.

It's a split-second decision to choose to tap into your insecurity. It seems easier and safer to live in the insecurity than to know we're worthy. Many people don't believe they are worthy of anything good in life. But that is just a story and it's simply not the truth. You wouldn't be here unless you were worthy. Whatever is fueling the insecurity needs to be identified because you are giving your power away. Once you know what the insecurity is, you need to work though it and eliminate it as soon as possible. Don't allow it to destroy your life or your relationships. Stop playing it safe and start living again. There is always a way to eliminate your insecurities. The real question is, are you ready to do the hard work? What are you going to allow to get in your way? Your answer has to be nothing. The answer *should* be "I will do the hard work and I will stop at nothing to achieve my worth."

Be warned—insecurities are difficult to let go of. The best way to let go is to dig deep, deep, deep inside and see your insecurities for what they are. Dig down to the root and uncover the insecurity. Replant beautiful seeds of truth around the old insecurities. Sometimes the truth about your insecurity is a reality and you need to fix the problem. Next, eliminate it and reclaim your power. Don't be afraid to stand up to your insecurity—you will learn so much about yourself and why it was created. You are always more powerful than you give yourself credit for.

Insecurities are incredibly painful and have a charge like nothing else in the world. It's important to figure out why you have the insecurity, where you got it, and how you got it. How did it become a permanent insecurity and why is it permanent?

When did you put your self-worth on the back burner and start letting your insecurities run your show? How do you plan to unravel your insecurity? Once you know the purpose of it, you will know where to go next. There are always hidden answers inside the things people call problems.

The question is, are you ready to share and let go? How excited are you to feel worthy again?

A huge side effect of an insecurity is that you pretend to be someone else. If you are acting like someone else to hide your insecurities, you are missing out and the world is missing out on you. Please be your true self and not your insecurities. Live in your worthiness and see how beautiful life can be.

12

FREE YOUR SELF-DOUBT WITH CONFIDENT DECISIONS

SELF-DOUBT

Self-doubt is defined as a lack of faith or confidence in oneself. Furthermore, one's actions, purpose, and/or abilities are brought into question when self-doubt comes into play. Self-doubt is fed by everything around you that makes you feel some type of lack. Self-doubt can be caused by media. Are you mindful of what you are watching and listening to? Are you aware of what you are absorbing?

Self-doubt is a persistent mental process that causes insecurities. It is a voice inside that is constantly questioning your decisions and choices; it is telling you they are wrong or worse, and it causes you to be indecisive. This affects your confidence and damages your faith in yourself. Let me ask you a question: If you don't believe in yourself, how will you find a life worth living for with passion and purpose? Can you take the step right now of wanting to believe, and then later in this section can you start believing in yourself?

Common self-doubt questions that people ask themselves usually starts with the "what if" game questions such as, what if I'm doing the wrong thing? What if I'm not enough? What if I can't do this? What if I'm not successful? What if I *am* successful? When you exhibit self-doubt, it means you don't believe in yourself, you don't have faith in who you truly are. People who doubt themselves are unwilling to risk believing in themselves out of fear. Have you ever truly believed in yourself? What are you so afraid of? When did you start having doubts about yourself, your decisions, and your ability to perform? Most importantly, why would you play the game of "what if" if you know it is destructive, devastating, and very unhealthy?

I want to take you back to my personal experiences with self-doubt that truly started when I was lying in the hospital bed after my surgeries. Imagine the self-doubt and feelings of dependency that started to arise while lying there scared and alone with an uncertain future ahead of me. The first time I felt self-doubt around my procedures was when I woke up and realized my life would never be the same because of a decision that I made—I would no longer be able to eat and exercise regularly; both were key aspects of my life. Imagine the overbearing self-doubt that came crashing down on me from those consequences that came with my decisions. If one decision can have that great an impact on the rest of my life, could I ever make a good decision again? Although at the time I didn't believe I could, I now know the truth to be yes, I can make great decisions, and so can you!

Typically, when going through self-doubt, you find yourself constantly thinking to yourself, "I don't know if I can do this," or, "I'm not sure if I'm enough." What should you do when you realize you are constantly doubting yourself? You have to make a choice to stop doubting yourself; start with just one thing and work one small piece at a time. As you begin to remove the self-doubt, start to fill the hole with confidence and personal growth. Just imagine who you are going to be when you become self-doubt-free. The power in knowing who I became after releasing my self-doubt, is honestly one of my best gifts yet!

WHAT FEEDS YOUR SELF-DOUBT MOST IS YOUR INNER CRITIC

You have a thought that you create and store in your mind. The idea is stored to help keep yourself safe from harm and suffering. This is what your inner critic tells you. In reality, the inner critic is often fighting to keep you where you are and stunt your productivity and growth. Your inner critic spoonfeeds your self-doubt. Common dialogue that occurs between you, your inner critic and self-doubt to look out for includes:

- "I'm safe where I am."
- "Change isn't that great."
- "I feel protected and supported now."

- "I'm not good enough."
- "I don't have to try anything new."
- "It's familiar and consistent."
- "You don't need change—you have me."
- "You'll never be good enough without me."
- "You can't do this alone."

You generally create these critics during your childhood years, but there are times you create them as an adult. When you create a critic as a child, its main job is to keep you safe. Often it is protecting you from ridicule, humiliation, and other emotional harm. But when you think about it, what do you honestly need safety from as an adult? You obviously need safety from physical harm, but that's not what a critic is trying to protect you from. A critic wants to protect you from embarrassment, and the best way to do that is to always stay the same, avoiding change and growth. As a child, you endured embarrassment and humiliation. To avoid repeating those unpleasant experiences, you remember the actions you took that led you to humiliation and vow to never repeat them again. Through this process, you begin to develop your critic. It is constantly in the back of your head telling you, "Don't do that!" or, "Don't you remember what happened last time you did that?"

Over time, you become comfortable with the critic's voice in your ear and even become friends and feel safe with it. However, our critics are often being overprotective. They close doors to new opportunities and stunt our growth. Once you stop listening to the critic and start making your own decisions, the critic no longer serves a purpose and can no longer whisper in your ear.

Critics come from your own self-doubt that sneaks into your thoughts, and they protect you even when you don't ask for help. Don't ever forget this: while they are there to protect you, they also have their own agenda to keep you down in the muck with them. Imagine you had a best friend all through childhood and you two were like bread and butter, always better together. You stayed the best of friends all through high school and then it came time to go to college. You went off to an out-of-state college, but your friend, not always the biggest fan of school, stayed home and started working. Four years went by, and when you returned from college you found that you and your friend no longer connected as well as you did before. You have changed a lot during your four years in college, but your friend is still very much the same person from high school. Your friend accuses you of changing during college and just wants to go back to the way things were before. However, you are happy with who you have become and proud of the growth you've experienced during your time away at college. You don't want to change back, but you might lose a friend if you don't.

This is an analogy is similar to the relationship you have with your critics. They want you to stay the same and keep living in the good old times you used to have. In reality, the critic is strapping you to a table and laying so much weight on top of you that you can barely breathe. It's difficult to grow under that kind of burdensome weight. This is the same type of friend a critic is. Is this the kind of friend you want to have in your life or would you prefer a friend who simply holds your hand and helps you get to the next level in life with no hidden agenda or judgment? If this sounds appealing but feels impossible, it's time to start working on your relationship with your critic and make confident choices for yourself.

Starve your self-doubt and fuel your inner confidence by no longer playing it safe with your old friend.

MY FIRST STEP IN OVERCOMING SELF-DOUBT

It starts with a choice to transform. The transformation must come one day at a time, through making one choice at a time and taking a leap of faith. For me, it started by making one decision: I am no longer going to sit on my bottom and live in pity and self-doubt. I am going to stop starving my faith in myself and begin starving the self-doubt instead. I made this choice in order to become the person I have dreamed of being.

First, I had to acknowledge my motivation and purpose, which was to help others, and my transformation took me from being a nanny to be a Life Coach. It started with having faith and trust in myself even though I was so scared. I knew I could do anything and be anything I wanted to be, but I was unsure how. I started by taking small steps in the right direction and taking action. I searched for a career that fed my inner desire to be more, and once I found it, I searched for schools. Once I found the school, I took another leap of faith, registered, and wrote the check. Enrolling in iPEC, I faced my fears and self-doubt head-on and made a vow to make the most of every minute I was learning.

Once you dip your feet in the water and take that leap of faith, you realize you can do anything! I took the leap and, at twenty-five years old, started my own company, Bringing Out The Best In You!, LLC. Now, how are you going to walk the talk like I did?

FREE YOURSELF FROM INDECISION

In life you will come across situations that will require you to make tough calls. There are times when postponing making a decision may seem like the easier thing to do, but you may be missing out on great opportunities because of your indecision. When you make the choice to be indecisive, you feed your self-doubt. Do not be wishy-washy with your choices. If there are any decisions in your life that have not been made, make them and avoid putting them off any longer.

The best way to free yourself is to make one choice at a time. It's important to trust yourself enough to exercise your power of choice. You've got this. You have to start somewhere—you can no longer live a life of indecision, trapped between two places. The more you work at being decisive and making choices, the less fuel your inner critic and self-doubt has. Now is the time to make confident strong decisions to free yourself from indecision and self-doubt.

BE BOLD ENOUGH TO MAKE YOUR OWN DECISIONS

Another common indicator of self-doubt is the willingness to allow other people to make choices for you. Often when dealing with self-doubt, you are unsure if you're making the right decision and you would rather have someone else make the decision for you. You are probably more afraid of making the wrong choice than of giving up the power to make the choice yourself. Just imagine what would happen if you allowed your mother to make every significant choice for you for an entire year. Would you still be living your life, or would you be living the life she chose for you?

This is not to say it's never a good idea to ask others for help or to work together. However, if you don't decide what you want first, how do you expect to know how you truly feel about the decision *without* the influential biases of others? When are you going to start living your own life based on your desires, not the desires of others? When is it your time to take over? When are you going to give yourself the chance to make your own decisions? Your time is now! When you are bold enough to make your own decisions, you will be bold enough to stand up to your self-doubt.

STOP MAKING DECISIONS FOR OTHERS

I used to think everyone around me knew better than I did when it came to big life-altering decisions such as medical choices. But when you really think about it, how would anyone know my health better than myself? How would you be able to help me with my health decisions without living in my shoes? By trying to make decisions for others, you take away their power and you may fuel their self-doubt and their inner people pleaser. If they want your input, they should and will ask. However, you should always lead people to make their own decisions because only they know what's best for them. You don't want to make choices for other people because the blame for how their life has turned out might fall on you. A decision made by someone who does not have a horse in the race may cause deep hurt for someone who does have something at stake. This is why you need to make your own decisions. If you lead others to make their own decisions, all parties will be happier, and your relationships will be so much stronger. You will be a true leader because leaders lead others to what is right for them.

In working with a variety of people through my coaching practice, I have seen that a tremendous amount of self-doubt is a common theme with the majority of people. The self-doubt shows itself in a variety of ways among the general public, and it affects everyone differently. As you recall, self-doubt is reflected in the way we talk to ourselves and ask questions.

Let's now review some common self-doubt stories and mental processes I have encountered with my clients. It really doesn't matter if you are five years old or sixty-seven years old—you have already had enough exposure to self-doubt because it is simply human nature and is a consequence of our blessed ability and choice to reason and think. The question is, how do my clients overcome their self-doubt? The answer is that they find someone they trust (whether it be family, friends, or a professional) to guide them through the pain and suffering of self-doubt to achieve emotional freedom. Self-doubt is a deep-rooted miscreant; don't be afraid to ask for help. I wrote this book to help you through your personal changes and challenges. You can think of me and this book as your family, friend and professional guide meant just for you!

While reading over the following stories from my clients, I would like you to think about how your own self-doubt may be similar to the stories. Take a moment after each story to think about whether something in the story really speaks to you and whether you can envision making the same transformational change that my clients have made.

STEVE'S CLIENT EXPERIENCE

Steve has been doing the same job for twenty years. He is fifty-one years old, and even after twenty years, he still believes he sucks at his job. Never mind the fact that last year he earned nearly six figures while working in sales. He was the top-grossing salesman in his company, which earned him the title of "Salesman of the Year." On top of that, he maximized the amount of money he could make as a salesman and won his dream trip to Alaska, simply because he works hard and is good at his job. Does that describe an individual who sucks at his job or someone who thinks he isn't good enough? What keeps him from believing in his own ability to perform a job he has worked for twenty years? How does a man like that start to believe in himself again (or for the first time)?

Steve and I needed start by really digging and trying to find the core of where his self-doubt lives. We needed to take an honest and reflective look into the past to see when he lost faith in himself and allowed the roots of self-doubt to take hold.

When Steve was about eleven, his parents divorced, and he had to move from a small town to the big city. As the young child he was, he didn't really understand what was going on. All he knew was that he missed his friends and family life. And that's when he started to doubt himself. Like many children, he was frozen in the thought that his parents' separation was his fault. His fears and doubts were feeding him the story that he would not make new friends. This was because he thought he would be moving back home. This was the fundamental place when Steve's "friends"—self-doubt and his inner critic—began guiding him through the next forty years of his life. (This is also where he started using fast food to numb his emotional pain.)

While this story may seem like a small thing to an adult, it only takes a single transformative change like this during your childhood to plant the seed of self-doubt that grows into a giant tree of self-doubt as an adult. Even the smallest thought of self-doubt can grow into something that hinders your belief in yourself and prevents you from recognizing your true potential. Although Steve is happily married with three beautiful children and has an amazing life, he spends the majority of his time doubting everything he does, always playing the "what if" game. He constantly asks himself if he is good enough and doubts his own choices because he lacks faith in his own system and beliefs.

So, how did Steve change his thought process and start to remove his self-doubt? Who do you think needs to tell him that he is enough? Should it be his boss? No. Does it help him if his boss tells him he is very good at his job? Yes, it does, but what if his boss never tells him he is good or bad at his job? Who else can he get these answers from? Where can he look? I encouraged Steve to look deep inside himself to figure out whether he truly believes he is good at his job. He needed to ask himself, *Do I really suck at this or is that just a story I am telling myself?* If he is honest with himself, he will know. I already know that the answer is "yes." I know he is great at his job because I have used his services in my own life and he did a great job. However, I can't convince him that he is good at his job, because he will never believe it. My words and opinions don't matter because if he doesn't trust himself, he'll constantly be in doubt of his abilities. One of the biggest reasons people have self-doubt is because they don't know their true selves or recognize their capabilities. They don't know who they are, and they don't know how to trust themselves, so they're constantly looking to others to fill that need.

Steve overcame his self-doubt by learning to stand up for his confidence. Once his confidence was on his side, he began to stand tall and have faith in himself, trusting he was good at his job, which overflowed into all areas of his life. This also helped defeat his self-doubt and silenced his inner critic. The best advice he can give to you is to stand up to your inner critic, no longer letting it steal your life away. Always live your life in the present moment and in the unknown. The freedom and happiness you will receive is priceless.

LARRY'S CLIENT EXPERIENCE

When Larry was five years old, his parents often fought at the dinner table. As a result, he would sometimes decide not to eat his dinner. His mother would explain that if he did not eat his dinner, he would never grow up to be big and strong and would be short and small for the rest of his life. It does not take many of these interactions for a thought process to embed itself into the psyche. Imagine what happened as he grew up and developed a value system based in self-doubt about his physical stature. Larry is very successful and at the young age of 26 is already a great doctor.

He recalls sitting with his parents at the dinner table and they would force him to eat. It made him sick to his stomach. He would stress out to the point where he would stop eating. As a result, he blames himself for being small, and he has created a thought process in which he unconsciously tells himself to skip his meals or he will get sick.

Is Dr. Larry small in stature because he skipped a few meals or missed out on eating his vegetables as a child? In all likelihood, no. It is much more likely that he is small because of his genetics. Of all people, one would expect a doctor to realize this, but because the self-doubt was ingrained as a child, his feelings about being small and insignificant trump his ability to reason when it comes to his size.

Give yourself a break. If a doctor can't see something this obvious, how would you be able to? Now that you can see how easy it is to miss self-doubt, how can you be aware of it?

After being shown the source of his self-doubt and doing some hard work, Larry has removed his self-doubt and begun to realize that his physical stature is not a reflection of his worth. His first step toward standing tall and confident inside was to feed the belief that he is good enough. The next step was to starve his inner critic. I confidently say that he is living a healthy life in which he is helping and saving people, free from self-doubt.

EVELYN'S CLIENT EXPERIENCE

Evelyn knew she was stuck in an area of her life and didn't know how to get out of it. She was working at a job that paid the bills, but it wasn't what she really wanted. However, due to her upbringing, she was doing what she needed to survive, whether she liked it or not. "Be grateful for what you have—you have enough" was what she was taught. Asking for more than the basic necessities was selfish, according to her upbringing. After coaching her for a while, I realized what her passion was, as it came out in our conversations. She thought she could try it part time but didn't quite have the confidence to go into it full time and quit her other job. She did take a step and went to school, which was really a refresher, as she had already been doing this for many years!

The good Lord gave her a little push and now she is working full time doing what she loves. There are still times she says to herself, "Maybe I should work for someone else. What if I can't pay my bills?" but she resists that critic, as hard and scary as it is to do. She continues to trust her decision and uses the tools from coaching because her new job is her passion and purpose. She now knows her true capabilities. She now gets up every morning and says "I am the best at my job and I will prosper in everything I do!" She has always believed in God, but now she has the faith to believe in herself!

I encourage you to determine the root of your self-doubt and find what is missing from your life; find out what is causing you to doubt who you are from the inside out. Most of the things that cause us to doubt ourselves are entirely created within our own minds based on present, past or future events. We keep the source of these doubts buried deep within us because we don't want anybody else to see our doubt. And you don't want to see the doubt yourself—you're afraid to look at it and pretend it doesn't exist. Evelyn says, face your problems, cowboy up, and work through them. Life is worth living without being afraid or doubting yourself. More important, learn from everything that has caused you pain or hurt. Surrender to God and trust in Him.

REPROGRAM YOUR SELF-DOUBT TO MAKE HEALTHY DECISIONS

So, let's start growing! Imagine you have a computer and you want the computer to do something different. You have to reprogram that computer, right? Well, same with your thoughts.

Start reprogramming your thoughts by following these guidelines:

- Remember that any time you let your self-doubt creep into your mind and allow it to become part of your thought process, it will continue to duplicate like a virus in a computer.
- Don't forget to have faith in yourself.
- Do everything you can to get out of your own way and become the person you want to be.
- Believe and visualize what it would be like to have freedom from self-doubt and everything holding you back.

- Even if you think it was the wrong decision, it's okay—that was your opportunity to learn.
- Create a healthy self-talk that allows you to be happy and fulfilled. This brain pattern will extinguish your self-doubt.
- Replace destructive thoughts with something you truly believe is good about yourself, even it it's not on the same subject. You have to be willing to build the truth. If you don't have one, create one and change.
- Create a list of the actions you will no longer allow self-doubt to sabotage. Then play the true-or-false game with each item on the list. If it's the truth, investigate how to change that so it can no longer be self-doubt. If it is false, then it's done, over with. Let it go! It isn't real, so create a pattern that is truthful and real for you.
- Remember, if you want to stay safe and sound, that is your inner critic talking—it doesn't want you to grow. Does it feel uncomfortable? If it feels comfortable, you need to make yourself a little uncomfortable and change the virus patterns.
- If it is not serving you, you can make the choice to get rid of it. Grab the bull, look him in the eye, and ask yourself, "Is this bull honkey?" If the answer is "yes," it's not serving you. Just let it go. If you look the bull in the eye, you'll see the truth, and once you see the truth, you can break it apart.
- Continue to do everything and anything possible to have faith in yourself and be free from your self-doubt.

HOW TO MAKE CONFIDENT DECISIONS A PRIORITY

Often, you can feel lost and unsure of what's going on around you. You don't know why you *are* doubting yourself; lots of times you are unaware that you are doubting yourself. On the other hand, there are times when you are fully conscious to your doubt, but you do not know how to get out. If you are the type of person who lacks the ability to make a confident decision, here is a perfect place to start.

The biggest and most important question to ask yourself is "How am I going to change my relationship with my self-doubt for the good?" One of the easiest ways to build your confidence is to start the process with something simple such as choosing pepperoni pizza over cheese pizza. Personally, I would go for the Hawaiian (hee-hee). It may seem silly, but many people struggle in making strong decisions even around their food. But it's as simple as looking at your two options, grabbing a slice of one or the other and moving forward without looking back.

Use simple choices like this to build confidence in your ability to make decisions, specifically for you and without regret. The momentum that builds from these small confident choices will help you to make strong, confident decisions at the more challenging forks in the road that are bound to appear in your future. You have to start somewhere, so you might as well start with one little slice at a time. If you are past one slice at a time, figure out where you need to start to build you confidence.

My own self-doubt manifested from my abusive childhood. From as early as I can remember, I was told l would never be enough, I could never be independent, I was stupid, worthless, and would never amount to anything significant in this world. I would overhear the adults in my life saying all these hurtful things due to their fears of my learning disabilities, dyslexia, and emotional baggage. For most of my life, these instances and situations built on one another and helped to fuel my self-doubt. However, they only fueled my self-doubt because I allowed them to and I did not know how to stop it.

When someone tells you that you are ugly, and you begin to see yourself in that way, you have allowed that person to create self-doubt. If before this experience you saw yourself as a beautiful person but now you see yourself as ugly, you have allowed an external factor to create internal self-doubt.

Take a moment to think about what happened in your own life that may have caused you to have self-doubt. I had a client with a tremendous amount of self-doubt that we worked on for several months before she overcame it. She had so much self-doubt that she was often asking herself if she would ever be enough. During our sessions, she would often ask, "Can I ever make a difference in this world again? Will I ever be good enough again?" While she asked me the questions looking for an answer, my only response was, "Why are you asking me?"

Maybe my client was looking for me to tell her something she wanted to hear. Maybe she wanted me to make the choice for her and tell her that, yes, she will make a difference in the world again and she is enough. And the truth is, at that moment I did know, but my place was not to tell her what I knew.

Instead, I guided her to realize and see a true understanding of who she is and what she has to give the world. Who am I to tell her how to live her life? Even if I did tell her she would make a difference again, what would it really mean? It would only have helped her in the moment. It would not have had any lasting impact, because she did not believe it herself. For a change to occur, she would have to come to the conclusion on her own. The conclusion that, yes, indeed, she will make a difference in the world again.

This is one of the fundamental principles of coaching and something I hold as a pivotal lesson in personal transformation. As your coach, I don't get to make choices for you, because I am not you. But I will do my best to guide and inspire you to make that choice for yourself. Do I think you can do it? Oh my gosh, yes! Do I have faith in you? Yes, of course! The gift that my Creator has blessed me with is unbinding faith in others; I have been blessed with the ability to see the best in people. So, yes, I have faith in you and believe in you. Unfortunately, I can't do your work for you. I don't have the power to face your inner critic—only you can. The journey is reserved for you, and I am here to replenish your strength as you travel along your path. I will give you the tools, the resources, and the accountability that you need to find your confident voice.

So once again, take a moment and look deep inside to figure out what has caused your self-doubt. What in your life has hurt you and caused you to lack faith in yourself? How will you turn it around? You are the only one who can answer these questions, because you are the only one who has all of the facts. If this is very difficult, it may be necessary to request the help of a professional. Please, never feel shame in asking for help. It makes your journey easier and faster.

The truth of the matter is, if you don't have the confidence and faith in yourself to make the decision, it really doesn't matter anyway. You have to rid yourself of the fear that you might make the wrong decision. Instead, ask yourself, *what if I make the right decision?* It often doesn't matter what choice you make. The right decision is making the decision in the first place. Your choices matter—own them regardless of whether the decision has difficult consequences or none at all. If you remove the consequences from the equation, you are no longer making choices at the effect of self-doubt. Decide for yourself. Be confident in what you choose, and you will find that in the long run, things will often work out, even if the journey is different from what you expected.

Now you have the choice to drown your inner critic. You are no longer a victim of the fear of the unknown. You are making the choice to take control of your decisions and your self-doubt. Don't ever be afraid to drown your self-doubt and replace it with confidence. It may be the best thing you've ever done.

BUILDING SELF-BELIEF

Self-belief is a beautiful emotion, feeling, and energy that comes from doing something you are passionate about and having a purpose. It can also come from simply believing in yourself and knowing you are capable of getting over whatever obstacle is in front of you. Self-belief takes a tremendous amount of trust, patience, wisdom, and presence. Self-belief is all about giving yourself the power and knowledge to get you to exactly where you want to go and what you want to do. Self-belief and confidence are one and the same; you cannot have one without the other.

How do we define confidence? In our society, confidence means feeling successful, powerful, and having no doubts. However, what it really means is to be certain in oneself. Once you can do that, you will be full of self-belief. Confidence is one of the hardest things to obtain because it is such a deep-rooted feeling. You should constantly have confidence. This will benefit your body, mind, and spirit.

Confidence is a way of life. It's all about choice; you have a choice to be confident, believe in your decisions, and trust yourself enough to eliminate the behaviors that don't serve you, such as self-doubt and snide comments from your inner critic. Have faith to go out into the world.

Know that when you lose confidence, it's only temporary. Confidence will become a part of you that no one can take away, including yourself. Confidence will become a recurring healthy pattern that will someday become permanent. Confidence can only make you stronger.

Imagine if you had self-belief and confidence every time you were about to make a decision. Imagine how much easier, happier, and healthier your life would be. Take a moment to decide how much you want the power of self-belief and self-confidence before you read the rest of this section. It is not easy to have a strong belief in yourself, so it is important to know how much you want the change.

Self-belief feeds you confidence and allows you to tap into your true potential. The purpose of self-belief is to keep you grounded and strong no matter what life throws at you. You will know you are in the right place at the right time, for the right purpose. Your inner faith will guide you to rely on this energy, emotion, and feeling to help you live a happy, healthy life.

One way to start building self-belief is to ask, *how can I fill that need for myself?* How can I start to give power to myself? Remember, this is all in your mind. Anything in your mind is changeable.

Building faith in yourself is not a simple flip of the switch. It is a process that requires consistent work and commitment. You have to make the decision to start—and to start with realistic goals. For example, if you want to lose forty pounds and get your high-school six-pack back, you can't go to the gym today and expect results tomorrow. Go figure! Building that six pack will take a consistent commitment to working out three to five times a week, changing your food relationship, and getting more sleep. You also have to understand that the results will come at their own pace, but if you stick with it you can have amazing results.

One strategy that works for weight loss is to take pictures along the way. The progress from day to day is often very slow, and sometimes you even go backwards. If you take pictures every two weeks and look back at the previous pictures, you will see significant progress. This tangible progress will help you build confidence and motivate you to get through the next two weeks. You can say that you love yourself now but you're excited to see your new stronger, lighter, healthier body.

You can use this weight loss philosophy for all parts of your life, including building your faith and self-belief. Building faith in yourself also takes consistent commitment and uncomfortable changes to your lifestyle, but if you approach it with a plan and understand that the results will come in time, you will be well on your way to building complete faith in yourself. If you make the decision to start trusting in yourself, in a few weeks or months you will be amazed at the progress you have made. By taking notes at the end of every week or two weeks of progress, you will be able to see just how far you've come.

I know sometimes you're shaking in your boots and you need a little bit of courage to get to your inner-confidence.

Find your inner-courage; it will help you build your self-belief. In the moments that you need it most, imagine that you are the strongest and most courageous person ever (which you are). Allow yourself to tap into your powerful emotion of courage any time you need a little extra. The simplest way to build self-belief and self-confidence is one thought at a time. Have faith in yourself with each thought. You have to build up your new skill and create a healthy pattern of encouraging the belief in yourself. Any time you have a negative thought about yourself, switch your thinking pattern to trusting in yourself. You have a couple of seconds afterward to think about something to change your pattern. It's not necessarily a fun game to play, but if you win it, you will never have to fight again.

Faith is everything when you are letting go of your self-doubt. Having faith in yourself starts as a seed that sometimes is watered by tears, hard work, and sweat. The seed was planted with the intention of making your dream to be full of faith come true. This is a place where only you can build yourself up by finding what is going to make you feel the most proud and confident in everything you do. When you find that inner faith, it starts to build into a beautiful tree that takes years to grow into a tree of faith. When you live in faith, fully trusting yourself and your Higher Coach, you know in your gut that you are doing the right thing at the right time. Eventually, you will have such blind faith in yourself that you won't even have to question if it's there.

Strive to find self-belief. Never give up.

13

CHANGING ONE STEP AT A TIME

ABANDONMENT AND LONELINESS

Abandonment and loneliness stem from your past or childhood. It also comes from people leaving you and making you feel like you are unworthy of their love and staying in your life. The people who leave you can be anyone: friends, family, or someone you've never met. When someone leaves you behind, it takes a huge chunk out of your heart and leaves you with shattered pieces of your heart to put back together. Some people try to fill their empty hearts by self-medicating or trying to meet their emotional needs by other people in inappropriate and unhealthy ways. Others distract themselves from the loneliness by throwing themselves into whatever will keep them busy and keep their minds off the pain that loneliness and abandonment bring into their lives. They will also deny that they need to be healed or that they even have a problem to begin with.

If you are one of the many people hurting from abandonment and loneliness, then this section of the book is written for you to show you how it has gotten in your way. I want you to be free from all the darkness and sadness that loneliness and abandonment bring.

What you do with the pain after you become a victim of being left behind is where the deep loneliness comes from, because you chose (unconsciously) to let the painful patterns keep going. People generally don't get healing in that area because they don't know where to go to release these horrible patterns and behaviors that someone showed them. Often, people who were abandoned are abandoning something or someone in their life, thus continuing the patterns or the polar opposite: clinging to anything and everything to fill the void. You may believe that it is normal to be left behind and that you deserve it, and no one wants you. However, I am here to tell you this is not normal, and you don't deserve that abandonment. Abandonment only occurs when you abandon yourself. If you never abandon yourself, then you will never have to feel abandoned or lonely again. You are enough.

Where the pain of being abandoned and feeling lonely comes from is easier to discover than it is to work through, because most of you know that you were left behind but aren't prepared and don't have the tools to let go. Because you have felt this way for so long, it has become natural for you to feel lonely and abandoned. You expect the world and everybody in it to leave you again and again. Many people are dealing with abandonment and loneliness and you would never know it. The feelings, abandonment and loneliness are hard to look at. The pain of abandonment is that deep, deep feeling that you get in your gut when someone leaves you or you leave someone. You are left with nothing to hold on to. Abandonment is that feeling where you have no one and nothing to rely on.

Loneliness is the biggest side effect of abandonment. It will smack you right in the face with deep darkness and sadness. Loneliness is that feeling that you won't have anyone who will ever love you or understand you. It makes you feel that you are unlovable and that this feeling will last forever that you will be alone forever because you feel as though you will never be good enough to be loved or worthy enough to stay for.

I want you to recognize what abandonment feels like for you, what it has done to you, and where in your life has abandonment caused you to be frozen in your emotional healing.

Abandonment is usually a deep-rooted issue that needs a lot of love and attention for healing to occur. The only way to heal is to give yourself that love, attention, and stability you needed and did not get from someone else. Abandonment really does make me sad.

A lot of my clients love to mediate or use imagery to go back to the time they felt abandoned. This may be a time when they were triggered, or this may be a time that they planned.

Start by asking yourself these questions: Is my mental, spiritual, and physical health ready for this kind of work. Am

I in a healthy place where I know I can have success in just guiding myself through this process? Am I strong enough? Will this be safe for me to undergo by myself? Is this right for me to do on my own or do I need a partner such as a coach or hypnotherapist because it's too much pain and fear for me to handle on my own? Am I ready to face the fear? Do I know I am in a safe place? Do I fully believe that it's the right time for me to work through this? You are the only one who can answer these questions.

I recommend planning a time-out and setting up the right space to do this. Create a safe and quiet place with relaxing, wordless instrumental or nature music. Take a couple of deep breaths.

As a hypnotherapist, I have my clients use a script I created for their healing needs titled "Own Your Loneliness and Abandonment." This imagery technique assists my clients in going back to the inner abandoned person who was left behind with only loneliness to hold on to.

If you're ready to begin the "Own Your Loneliness and Abandonment" script, start by closing your eyes taking a couple of deep breaths. Continue those breaths while relaxing your whole body. Start at the top of your head and go all the way down to your toes, focusing on each individual body part at a time. Many imagine their favorite safe place as an environment for their mind frame to be in as they are going back to that moment as a strong individual who is there to help the inner abandoned person/child. They are seeing that inner abandoned person in front of them or beside them with the goal of showing that abandoned person that they are not alone and that they will be healed from the pain now that they see they have a true partner (you in the now) to heal with. If you choose to use this technique, I highly recommend that you think and say aloud, "I am a loving, lovable person who deserves love and I am capable of receiving love. But do more than say it—believe it!

Maybe you have someone who you trust, and love join you on your healing path. Some people grab their abandoned selves by the hand and tell that inner person "I've got your hand and I've always got your back," "I'm never going to leave you like everybody else did," and, "I'm so sorry that I have never shown you that I am here with you and I will be with you till the end of time."

If my clients are spiritual, I have them bring in their spiritual partners. For example, some choose to bring in God and I show them that God loves them unconditionally and that God will never abandon them or leave them. He is always with them in their hearts. For some, it is easier to imagine a loved one who they admired and trusted who has passed on join them on their journey of healing. I also have my spiritual clients, or anyone willing to try something outside of the box, grab on to those wonderful spiritual things or persons and imagine that their Higher Coach, whoever that may be, is wrapping them with a handmade blanket and armor of protection, unconditional love, and stability.

When experiencing hypnotherapy, some of my clients choose to heal by telling off the person who left them and telling their abandoner that they are better off without them. This technique is about moving past the feelings of lonliness to finally feel whole again. It's about filling that void with the truth.

But more importantly, it's about showing yourself that you have the power to be happy and you don't need other people to make you feel happy—all you need is yourself for this technique. You can repeat this method to heal your abandonment wound and other wounds, too. It may take more than once to break the pattern so don't be afraid to use this technique in new ways as long as it's still in a safe environment.

The hardest part of this technique is being able to let go, to forgive, and to trust again. Don't allow that experience to affect your future and present life. It was their choice to leave you. I know that it is incredibly painful to take in that someone didn't see how beautiful you are, and I am sorry they left you. Luckily, you do have a choice in all of this now.

So, what is your choice? If I could choose for you, I would choose for you to stand tall in your loneliness, to let go of it and know you are a loving, lovable person who deserves love and is capable of receiving love. If I could, I would also choose for you to never abandon yourself and always give yourself all the love you have to give. My dream for you is that you will love yourself so much that you are overflowing with it. So that someday, you continuously give love to others in a healthy way. You can't give love if you don't first let go of your abandonment. If you have no love and you are full of loneliness, how are you supposed to give someone something you don't have? It's impossible. It's ingenuine if you try to love with emptiness in your heart. If you can dig really deep, believe you're worth loving, and are prepared to let go of the longing for the love from the person or people who have abandoned you, you are ready to start letting go and begin your beautiful healing process. To begin your healing process, you can use the "Own Your Loneliness and Abandonment" script provided for you above or listen to the vocalized script that can be found on my website at Bringoutu. com.

I'm sorry to play devil's advocate in showing you both sides of the story, but I'm coaching you through both sides for a reason: healing purposes.

Remember that the person who hurt you feels the burden they put on you. I know you don't want to hear that, and you have probably avoided it at all costs. I know it's incredibly unfair of me to ask that, but when I finally looked outside of myself with humility, I understood that there is more to the story, as there always is. I think that it is okay for me to ask you to do this after I have done it myself. However, as always, the choice is yours.

When you can look outside of yourself, it allows you to see the big picture that you are not alone in your pain anymore. The person who hurt you may not feel the same pain and loss as you, but they feel some pain from leaving you. They may never tell you or show you, but it's always there, acting out in one way or another. Please be willing to forgive and get out of your own head and your own problems. This will help you forgive because seeing the abandoner as human makes the abandoner someone real, someone who has feelings, someone harder to hate, someone you can understand to some degree, and someone who feels human pain, just like you. It is so important to forgive the abandoner. If not for them, then for you.

Focus on forgiveness for yourself so that you can heal yourself. Make it an added bonus to be able to give someone else the gift of forgiveness. Forgiving someone else is incredibly difficult! Ask yourself, is it easier to put your efforts into a grudge or is it more rewarding to work toward healing for yourself and others? If you don't forgive, you spend so much time in heavy, unhealthy energy, wasting your energy when it's so much healthier to work on forgiveness. Beware that your mind will always go to the negative first; don't let it. I think it is easier to forgive in the moment and work through your pain in the present than it is to allow it to drain you in the long run.

(Abandoner: Now that you know about abandonment and you know the heartache it brings, please know that the guilt you must feel is so heavy, and the burdens you are carrying must feel like a bag of bricks on your chest. Fortunately, you, too, can have the blessings of healing. You can use the above steps as well, by imagining going back to the person you left behind to tell them your side of the story, apologizing, and showing them that you will be there for them from now on. This technique works if the person is alive and does not want you in their life or if the person has passed on, because the commitment to be with them is for yourself.)

Start by knowing your love for yourself. Be bigger than the loss you feel inside.

You are stronger than you give yourself credit for. Let this be the time to give yourself credit. Let this be the time to take action and stay focused. Don't let anything get in the way of your freedom from the incredible darkness that loneliness has placed in your life. If you are willing to look in the world or the universe for unconditional love, look above to your Higher Coach, or whatever spiritual coach you have, and find that love for yourself. Know that there is so much love out there for you to grab on to because this world is so much bigger than you and me. You are never alone. There is always someone else out there hurting and feeling something similar to you. Please don't allow your mind to tell you that you're all alone and that no one understands. That's exactly how your mind keeps you in loneliness: by telling you that you are all alone and by isolating you. Be bigger than the abandonment you feel inside, because you deserve to be free. You deserve to be loved. Stand outside of your loneliness and abandonment to see who you really are.

HOW THE PAST HOLDS YOU BACK

As you surely know, I had lots of pain and suffering rooted in my past, as many do, including my clients. After I did my work, the pain of my past has given me wonderful, spiritual advantages in the world. This pain and suffering have truly helped me understand my gift and taught me how to use my talents in this world. My story was hindering to the point where I felt limited, suffocated, and defined by who my past/childhood said I had to be and who I will be become.

Many wonderful people have pasts that have helped them do amazing things in the world. However, those people have done their needed work. Without doing your work, your past usually brings you down, keeps you from being your true self, and can prevent you from being seen in the light you are meant to shine in.

You can't change and still hold on to your story. You must give up your story first, with the faith and the understanding that you will get an incredible gift in return: the truth of who you really are without your defining past. The past will no longer have the controlling power of defining who you are or creating the expectations of who you will become. It will just be the past, no energy, simply the pure truth of what happened and what it taught you.

You will have to be alone without anything to define you. It will take immense strength to stand in that uncomfortable void of nothingness. Don't be afraid of what the fear of being without a story may tell you, because this void is remarkably educational and self-awakening. Take the opportunity to stand in the void and learn from it. That fear is telling you that you are close to being free and that you are on to something. You will learn how your story is meant to be used and you will be able to use it accordingly. This is how your past holds you back. If it wasn't a little bit scary, how would you know if it's something worth taking a risk in letting it go of?

People don't usually realize that their current, normal behaviors or struggles with their lives have generally stemmed from their past and spawned a new tree in their adult lives. We have allowed our past to have control and power over our entire lives.

It's difficult to recognize on your own where your deep-rooted unhealthy behaviors came from. These behaviors are poisonous in our lives. We take that pain or unknown destructive behavior with us into our adulthood, not realizing we can let go of it and change it, leaving all the bad in the past.

You feel such a deep connection to the past. You feel habitually safe with your past—it's all you've ever known. So, of course, it defines you because you don't know anything else. You can't see outside your past. You've created your identity, character, and behavior from everything that you have gone through and everything that has influenced you.

Your past does not have power over your life like you tell yourself it does. I want you to be able to realize you gave your past the power to control your happiness and your peace. Even if you were a victim to it the first time, that does not mean you need to continue giving your past fighting fuel. It can be very scary to grow when you have never lived without that past identity, that pain, that crutch, those excuses, and the story you tell other people.

I know it's hard to be told you have created more problems and drama because of what you have taken from your past, but if you are willing to look beyond the past, you can see who you will become without the story from your previous circumstances. (Keep in mind that there are experiences that are so horrific and devastating that it will take a different kind healing. Those are not the circumstance that I am teaching you to let go of.)

There are some steps you can take, as a gift for yourself, if you are fully ready to understand how your past has gotten in your way. If you are ready, please find a quiet place without distractions. Do the following if you truly want to heal from your deep wounds and hurt from the past. Look deep into your past or childhood and think of all that was done to you, said to you, and taught to you. Take a deep breath. Bring in one pain point at a time to see what behavior patterns it has helped you create. Now that you see it, you have the opportunity to go through it, learn from it, and throw it away.

Take action by getting rid of anything that is hindering you. Don't hold on to anything unless you are incapable of letting go on your own. It all depends on how badly you want your freedom and if you are ready to be free from your past. Stay aware and find anything and everything to help you be free from this horrible weight that has restrained you.

When you have made the time and the space in your life for your work that needs to be done, self-explore by writing out the answers to the following questions:

1) What deep-rooted childhood or past experiences or thoughts are you covering up? Now that you're looking at them, what do you need to do with them? How do you plan on letting them go and living without them?

2) How deep do your roots go? (If they go too deep, it would be wise to seek outside help.) How tall is your tree of troubles from what you have experienced? You can overcome anything if you are willing to not give up and give it the work it needs.

3) Are you aware that your past has caused problems that exist right now?

4) Now that you know what has gotten in your way, what are you going to do about it?

5) Are you prepared to dissect each memory and choose to let it go? If you are, prepare yourself for the work that is needed. Know that if you are ready to let it go right now, you can just let it go. If you're not ready to

let it go in this moment, that's okay. It just means that you need more time and possibly a partner to talk it through with, someone without an agenda.

6) Are you ready for the emotional roller coaster of the release from the pain of the past, the strain it will put on you, and the temporary exhaustion it will cause?

7) Are you ready for the freedom, the lifting of the weight, and the positive resultsof letting go of your past?

8) Who are you without your past, all the stories, drama, chaos, and distractions that hold you back? You may feel like you're nothing and as though there is nowhere for you to go. But I assure you, your walk on your own will create strength and understanding of who you are without your past. You may take a different approach to this question and use positive thinking in writing: I am smarter, happier, or calmer without my past. You want to be able to stand strong knowing that you changed your life without letting your past define your success, now and in the future. In the end you can be positive, motivated, and proud of who you are and look forward to who you will become.

This is simply a start to digging up the roots from your past in order to grow a new healthful tree of who you are without the energy around your past.

Most of the time, we need help to see what energy we have taken from our childhood or past that may be holding us back in the now. Don't be afraid to seek a professional to help you heal yourself. We all need help. It's worth asking and finding a supportive partner who drives you to be free from your past pains, thoughts, and experiences.

This growing process will take time, patience, and kindness toward yourself. Also, this change will require the shedding of blood, sweat, and tears from the release of emotions. With your new awareness you can begin to let go—one painful memory at a time.

OWN YOUR BAGGAGE

Everything you carry from your past, present, and future is considered baggage. Every negative life experience, big or small, affects you; it eventually adds up to our personal baggage. Most of the time your baggage is a combination of all your pain and struggle summed up in one huge heavy sack that you cannot bear to carry, but is attached to you at all times, sometimes without your knowing it. You think if you suppress it, it will go away. Unfortunately, suppressing your baggage will only increase its power and take more power away from you. Most of my clients have uncontrollable anxiety because they have ignored their baggage and haven't work through it.

Every day that you carry your baggage is another day that your baggage gets to drain the life out of you. You forget the consequences of not working through your baggage and you throw it to the side to ignore it (yet still lugging it around) like its no big deal. I want you to do everything you can to unloadall your baggage that has created emotional pain. Make today the day that you work through your baggage and leave it behind.

The best way to work through your baggage is to go through it one piece at a time, healing it, giving it awareness and understanding. You also need to look at the cords that are connected to your baggage and cut them off. Sometimes you need to just set your baggage down, leave it, and never look back.

This next part explains how to help others go through their baggage. The best way to be there for someone hurting and sharing emotional pain is by not getting into their baggage completely and not stuffing it into your sack. It's easy to get sucked in, but please don't take responsibility for someone else's pain, because you already have a heavy sack. You can get stuck in other people's baggage like its quicksand, so be careful. The best thing you can do is to give them space where they feel heard, understood, and loved without you getting all the way in it with them.

Sometimes when you are going through someone else's baggage, you get triggered into your own baggage. This is not good, because if you are triggered in your baggage, you are not being present in helping the other person and it becomes about you.

Always have one hand holding their hand for support and comfort, but you must keep your other hand for yourself, holding on to your freedom and your truth. This will keep you from getting lost in others' emotional pain and experiences. Own your baggage, stay out of others' baggage, and enjoy a life where you're not weighted down by your sack.

14

GAINING YOUR FREEDOM STEP-BY-STEP

BE YOUR OWN SAVIOR, NOT SOMEONE ELSE'S ENABLER

There are many types of saviors, but we are only going to talk about two types of saviors, primarily the unhealthy form.

The savior that I will rarely talk about is the healthy type of savior. The form of savior that we all strive to be, someone who truly does good for others, out of complete selflessness, not expecting anything in return, with no underlying motive. This type of savior is one of the most admirable, beautiful, courageous saviors, creating powerfully moving, tearjerking moments in our lives that shift us in a new direction. If you are this rare type of savior, thank you so much for sharing your light and love in this world. Only saviors like this should save. Don't try to be a savior unless you can commit to standing in the power of being truly selfless.

If you are the other type of savior, like I was and some of my clients were and most of our world is, then this section is made for you. You will know which savior you are, based on your motives, whether it be to help others or to feel good about yourself.

The type of savior that I'll be focusing on is someone who feels empowered and loved and plays the hero by always saving someone else. This type of savior feeds off the energy and praise of those they are attempting to save. Painfully enough, they are often unconscious to the fact that they are hurting the ones they are trying to save. Being this type of savior often *enables* others and does not allow any room for either parties' growth, change, or independence. This form of savior is not only a selfish savior but also a distraction to others (and themselves) from the importance of loving and taking care of themselves first.

Have you ever thought about why you're attempting to save others? Likely, the initial idea is that you're helping someone, which sometimes can be true, but in this form of saving that is not the case. Acknowledge the truth, whether it be that you are helping or hindering that person. Can you see what saving others has kept you from doing in your life and in their lives? You may be tempted to continue saving because it makes you feel good about yourself. Refrain from the temptation of saving others. Before you take care of others, you must take care of yourself. Self-love is extremely important.

The healthiest way to help others is to guide them to their own truth so they will be able to save themselves. I know you love to give advice and share your wisdom, but others need to gain their own wisdom. The best way to help others is to ask specific thought-provoking questions that guide them without giving the direct answer.

If you are this type of savior, stop killing the growth of others just because it is more comfortable to keep saving them than finding a new solution to your own problems and making a change. When you're strong and ready, you will have the ability to guide others in saving themselves because of your understanding of the importance of allowing others to fall and learn from their own trials and tribulations. You will allow others to be able to take charge of their own destiny and learn from their own emotional pain so that they may become emotionally resilient.

Be aware of the traps that you could get caught in when saving others. Savior energy is sneaky in making you feel good about yourself. Remember, once you see what that tricky savior energy does, you will realize that you cannot in good conscience keep saving others. Keep your eyes wide open and watch other people grow on their own. The destination is their choice; people have the choice in life to grow or not to grow. Don't be afraid to fall or allow the people you love to fall. There is learning in everything for you and them.

I say no thank you to this type of saving. I don't want your help. I want you to save yourself so that the person you are trying to save can save themselves, too. If you don't believe you need saving from saving, at least recognize why you are saving others and what you are doing to them by restraining their growth.

I definitely admit to creating unhealthy saving energy in my life before I became a Life Coach. I was taught to show love and to feel love by saving and helping others in an unhealthy way. For many years, I wrongly believed it was a positive gesture. The pure truth is that I didn't know any better; I was taking the power away from both of us (me and whomever I was saving). I would bet that you are like me, and I know that this is a hard truth to face. I'm sure you thought that your intentions were good, and so does everybody else, myself included. The truth is, you are hurting and enabling the other person, so now is the time to grow and change.

Growing up with a mother who was terrified, needy, insecure, and lonely, not to mention unstable, gave me a first-class ticket to be a personal (unhealthy) savior. This gave me the exclusive on how to be just like her. I unconsciously learned the pattern of feeding her insecurities and her loneliness, which gave me a magic ticket to her never leaving me because I was the one fixing her, helping her, and saving her. This is how enabling causes false security and creates unhealthy, toxic codependent relationships.

Being around someone who was supposed to be my role model and ended up acting as my mother did showed me that if I was just able to save her, I would feel love from her, safety, and motherly comfort in knowing she would never leave me because I fixed her, I saved her. It felt so good to think I was fixing her life and her problems. Unconsciously, I thought saving her would make me a good person and a good daughter.

I thought that my mother would finally have enough room in her life and would finally love me if I fought hard enough. I honestly thought that if I saved her, she would choose me over the drugs.

This behavior pattern she taught me seeped into my life relationships like a wildfire. She showed me to be not only the (unhealthy) savior but also a people-pleaser. At that time, I thought this was the only way to receive love from the one person I wanted it from most. Imagine how hard it was for my coach, Kerri, and me to put out the roaring, virtually untamable wildfire that was burning in my mind for years.

In the moment, I honestly thought I was helping my mother by trying to do her needed work for her, but in the long run I was doing it for me. Unconsciously, when I was a little girl and my biological mother was sober, I would tell her how to live her life. More specifically, I oversaw her banking and I balanced her checkbook on a weekly basis. I planned out every penny that she was to spend, just to help her understand the value of money and the relationship she should have with it. I wanted her to succeed so badly. I saved her to have a better life, so she could be in my life. I saved her because I felt so sorry for her, because she looked like a sad, hurt little puppy, and I was terrified to turn out like her. I saved her out of fear. Of course, as a child, I saved her because I loved her unconditionally and I wanted the same in return. It can be so deeply rooted and ingrained in your mind. If you are thinking that there is no way you are doing this, it may need a deeper look. Do yourself a favor—look deep inside your life and find the ways that you are saving and enabling. You will have to be vulnerable to do this;

you will have to hush your inner critic. Once you do this, you will be so happy being free.

Pause here. Take three deep, slow, relaxing breaths. Think of a time in your life that you had false security in a relationship due to saving. Now that you can see all the damage that you have caused in codependent relationships, you can learn from your past. You can ensure that you will not continue these patterns in the present or in your future. Take action to replace your old patterns with new healthy ones.

The best way to stop unhealthy saving is to be aware of who you are trying to save as well as why you're doing this. It is pertinent to stop these behaviors the moment you catch yourself doing it. Luckily, once you see it, you can't unsee it. If you remain focused on saving yourself, you will never feel the need to engage in unhealthy saving again.

You're worth loving! You are worth saving! You crave all the love and attention you're giving away through saving. You need to give it to yourself, especially before you can give it away. It's just like on an airplane, where you must put your own mask on before helping others around you. You should always start by filling yourself up with the love you're giving away. The people you're saving need to do the same for themselves.

VOICELESSNESS

Voicelessness is a feeling that you can't speak, that you are limited, that you have a lot to verbally contribute but feel like it's not worthy of being shared. It's like having chains around your vocal cords. It is as though there is a piece of duct tape over your mouth and you can't speak. If there was something good to say, you would be too paralyzed to say it.

I have felt voiceless my whole life, especially with my learning disability. My problems with reading, writing, and spelling are by far the most difficult learning disability I deal with on a daily basis. As an adult, it's gotten a lot harder especially because I own a business and help run many others. At times, this book was a very voiceless process for me. I feel that I can't always explain to others what I am trying to say.

For example, I have had a tough time with the employees I have hired to type for me while I am creating this book. My biggest problem is that they don't always understand what I am trying to say or the point I am trying to convey.

The other tools I'm using also are paralyzing as well. Tools such as computers and iPads that read to me. Well, let's just say that at times it's hard and makes me feel like my voice isn't strong enough to speak. On the other hand, I am very grateful for both: the people who helped find my voice in the book and the devices that help me feel less limited as an author who has dyslexia.

The really cool thing about having a learning disability or feeling like you don't have a voice is that you can find your voice while overcoming the limitations in the moment when you most feel voiceless.

I share my voiceless challenge with you to give you a better understanding of what it is like to be voiceless. Here are some questions to answer in getting your voice back.

I am talking about everyday voicelessness. Are you aware of all the times you have not spoken up and you wish you did? Of course, you are.

How often do you have the feeling that you can't speak, and you have nothing good to say?

Have you ever had the feeling of duct tape over your mouth? Next time you have this feeling, what will you do to take off the duct tape and speak up?

Do you ever just feel paralyzed? If you have, what can you do differently now to move? You have all the power to move, no matter how big a problem you're going through.

Do you still need to say those things, or can you let them go?

Do you know you do have something good to say and it's worth saying? You do have something good to say, and don't let anyone take that from you! Why would you wait to say something?

What held you back in the past from speaking up? Whatever it is, don't let that be the reason you feel like you have no voice. Say what you need to say with respect and kindness. Don't hold back. Now is the time to stand in your power and use your voice.

Alli's Voicelessness

Above I talk about being voiceless in everyday life. The story I'm about to share with you is about being voiceless in a totally different way, in the sense that is beyond extreme. Alli's story is one where someone or something takes your voice away from you and you can't stop it. Severe cases of voicelessness are incredibly hard to overcome and can take years or even decades to heal.

Going through this extreme voicelessness is all about grieving through it, temporarily surviving, and getting as much help as you can to heal from it. It's also about finding a way to turn your voicelessness into purpose. When dealing with intense cases of voicelessness like the client story that follows, a therapist/medical expert can be beneficial and even necessary. I believe that the more support you can get, the better off you will be when it comes to this type of silence. Healing from this is really a case-by-case thing. This story is here for all those voiceless victims in the word who want freedom and need the inspiration to find a way to achieve it. I am hoping that this can help you find the freedom and peace you so desire!

My client, Alli, is a mom of three kids and a survivor. Her story is one of the most extreme cases of losing the ability to speak physically, mentally, and emotionally that I have seen with such an extraordinary turnaround; Alli's story is one where she became voiceless and then freed her inner victim.

Her now-ex-husband's uncle—we'll call him Bobby—showed up on her doorstep on Halloween. Even though Alli was a little hesitant, because she had never been alone with him, she let him inside.

Her two little boys, who were almost one and two and half years old, were sitting in their high chairs while eating lunch. Alli and the kids were going to go trick-or-treating after they finished eating.

The first twenty minutes of Bobby's visit were okay. However, sometime after that initial twenty minutes, Bobby put Alli's phone in his pocket. For no real reason, things escalated. He pulled a gun on Alli and shoved it into her stomach. Bobby demanded cooperation from Alli. At this point, the kids were screaming in horror out of fear for their mama. Alli explained that she will never forget that frightful sound.

Against all efforts by Alli, Bobby aggressively handcuffed her. She managed to temporarily escape multiple times, but to her dismay, Bobby caught her through all her attempts. He tackled Alli and wrapped something around her neck and tightly tied it; this caused Alli to "pass out." When she woke up, she was completely out of it. She recounts that she tried to get on her feet, but she stumbled. She was too weak to stand.

He had to keep tackling Alli because she wasn't cooperating; she kept fighting back. Eventually, Bobby told her he would hurt, even kill, her sons if she didn't do exactly what he said. The mama bear in Alli was unwavering; he was not going to touch her kids! So, she got in the truck to protect her cubs.

Observant Alli noticed a few things when she looked in the truck: women's clothing, which would fit him and not Alli, sex toys, and pliers. It was at this point that Bobby's intentions with Alli became crystal-clear.

Alli brings me to inspirational tears for many reasons. One of the biggest reasons is her ability to be so present in a difficult situation, which allowed her to stay calm and not panic, as many people would if they were in her shoes. Her choices and resilience allowed her to use her voice to negotiate her freedom, save her life, and even get Bobby to drive her home. She saved herself in the face of a life-or-death situation. She never gave up, because she made the in-the-moment choice that she was going to live.

Finally, brave Alli escaped and called for help. Alli explains that the emotional, mental, and physical bruises and wounds she suffered were unlike anything she has ever experienced. Her neck was unrecognizable from the strangulation; she illustrated how excruciating it was for her to look at herself, let alone love herself.

The days, weeks, months, and years after that dreadful Halloween day were beyond difficult. Alli went to court for two and a half years; she fought very hard for justice. Her ex-husband would rarely come to court with her. The time that he did, he told her to stop being so greedy and take the ten-year plea deal. Alli was silenced by her ex, his family, their friends, and the people in Bobby's immediate circle. Alli says she never understood why they didn't rally behind her to love on her and support her. This made her feel even more voiceless, rejected, and abandoned.

Not only was her voice silenced, but so were Alli's pleas for support through PTSD (post-traumatic stress disorder), anxiety, depression, and the plethora of other terrible feelings she experienced. All the emotions and her label of being a victim to circumstances were new to Alli, but they were so real. She discovered quickly that she had extreme triggers and a lot of emotions to work through and let go of.

The day of Bobby's arraignment, Alli read her statement to the judge. The entire time she was telling her story to Bobby. Alli explains how speaking her truth, especially to Bobby, was the hardest thing she has ever done, but this is where she started to get her voice back. She knew that she had to tell her truth, no matter how difficult it was to express. Rightfully, Alli ended up winning the case; Bobby is now serving twenty-five years. Speaking her truth and standing in her truth are some of the ways she healed herself, freed herself from being a voiceless victim, and let go of what happened to her.

Alli expresses that feeling voiceless empowered her to improve herself, grow closer to God, shout her story from the rooftops, and discover new healthy relationships. It took a long time to remove the toxicity from her life on her own and through coaching. Alli says she is no longer lost in a lonely world. She explains that learning to grow through these pains has been life-changing. She even says she does not for one second regret what happened to her on that Halloween day.

Alli has fought relentlessly to become the incredibly strong woman who focuses on growth. She uses her story to advocate for herself, other women, her daughter, and others like her who have also been silenced, been victims, and felt voiceless. She explains that she has learned that even at the end of the bad days, there is still good in the world and a difference to be made in someone's life. She had to lose everything to become who she is today. Despite all the loss she has experienced, Alli and I are so proud to say her voice is louder than ever.

As a coach, I marvel at Alli's strength, courage, growth, and willpower. She empowered herself, by herself, without support (except from Jesus). When she met me, she had already started to move on from her horrendous experience and regained her voice. She was on her way to freeing her inner victim and much more. It was so inspirational to see how she did so much work on her own. That being said, there was still work for us to do to help her become the woman she wants to be and to have the freedom she deserves.

When I meet Alli, I was blown away that she made the choice on how to handle her nightmare of an experience. I was also impressed with how Alli was her own savior and she didn't let anything enable her in her quest for her voice and personal growth. Alli and I worked on her triggers, relationship coaching, boundaries, and general therapeutic listening. Alli's story about overcoming victimhood and letting go of her voicelessness should encourage everyone to make the choice to free themselves from it through self-healthing in a natural and healthy way. If anyone feels like they can't get through their voiceless nightmare, I hope you know that you are not alone, and people are there to help you heal through it. Make today the day you speak up, free yourself, and become a leader like my client Alli did, and if you choose to, you will, too.

FREEING YOUR INNER VICTIM

Freeing yourself from your inner victim is challenging. I hope you say, "Challenge accepted," because I know you can conquer what has trapped you. Victimization turns you into a cold stone statue leaving you unable to live or move on.

You have the ability to choose how you are going to act and be. That freedom is priceless. Put your freedom to good use.

Always choose to be victorious over your circumstances. Life will be an easier lesson to learn from if you are willing to sit in your victimhood from the get-go.

A victim is someone who is hurt either mentally, physically, or emotionally by themselves or others and could not find a way to escape or become unparalyzed from the uncontrollable circumstances that have happened to them. A victim is also someone who can't see any way out, making them feel like they don't have a choice in being a victim. A victim is someone who is lost in their story and has tunnel vision, making them focus on what happened and not how to free themselves from it.

A victim can feel tricked and helpless. They feel damaged and destroyed by what happened to them. Victims feel punished. Victims are incessantly in fear-filled survival mode of fight-or-flight. There is a constant dreadful thought that the incident that caused the victimization will happen again. Being in a crisis mind frame is extremely exhausting. Many victims feel a need to fight their way through life because fighting for what they want, or need has been the only way they have ever received what they are looking for. Fighting for what you need quickly becomes a habit that turns into a pattern. Your mind thinks you have to fight for every single thing you want in life, and now you become a permanent fighter.

Being a victim is such a hard thing to comprehend and own because you so often think that being a victim means you have gone through or have seen something tremendously horrible. You think being a victim is being raped or abused, and by all means those exploits do label you a victim. However, you may be unaware that you can also be a victim to your own thoughts, beliefs, fears, behaviors, actions, emotions, events, and situations; this type of victim is the one I am addressing in this section.

I want to make something abundantly clear: Tragedy does strike, and it is horrendously devastating. If you have experienced something in the realm of rape, abuse, or torture or someone was taken from you, I encourage you to seek outside help. I highly recommend that you never stop looking for your healing, because you are probably stuck where your devastator/attacker left you. Recognize that just because they left you there doesn't mean you have to stay there. I know it's hard to look at, but if you stay where they left you, you're still giving them your power. Please, for yourself, do everything you can to step outside of what happened to you, because it is so important to see that there always is a life worth living.

Of course, if you are the type of victim who went through that kind of intense tragedy or went through something unspeakable and unfathomable, take what you need from this section. Even though it was not written for the tragic type of victim specifically, the people who have gone through the extremes may be able to use some of this section to heal or use this part of the book to help with a different time that they were a victim.

We often have experiences that leave us trying to wish pain out of existence, even though you can't. You have to approach your victimhood head-on and work to eliminate it. What can you do to learn how to handle your life circumstances more effectively, so you feel less of a victim? The best way to handle what life throws at you is to be present and in the moment.

Work through your circumstances then and there. Don't put off them off until a rainy day; today is your rainy day. Take your incidents as they come so that they don't pile up into a muddy mess. Once you deal with the rain and the storm, you will be delighted to find the light of the rainbow.

You can't avoid the feelings and emotions associated with being at the effects of victimhood. It happens to everybody. It's a huge part of life, and what you do with it is completely up to you. The hurt from victimization is a crucial part of our learning process, so embrace it. When it comes to victimization, you can always find meaning in your pain.

There are multiple types of victims in this world, but the main purpose of learning about victimhood is to overcome emotional victimization and the pain that holds you back. Being a victim myself, I had a difficult time facing the truth that I needed to let go of my label, my pain, and my story of being a victim. I often felt like others would view me as weak if I moved on or if I needed to talk about it. I was afraid of talking about being a victim, because I thought it would give the victim story more power. Like many of my clients, I did my best to avoid being a victim. You must lean into everything that isolates you as a victim to be able to take your power back.

Be patient. I know that sounds impossible, and that's exactly how I felt, too. I am here to say that with hard work and deliberate dedication, it is possible to be free from the victim story of what happened to you.

It is important to prepare yourself for the side effects of an emotionally draining release. Create a game plan for recharging yourself so you can continue releasing the feelings and emotions of victimhood. Take a deep breath and jump into deciding if you want to be free from being a victim. It's so incredibly liberating. Try it on. See how it feels to be free.

Please understand that this is my point of view upon reflecting on my own and my clients' experiences. Everyone's circumstances are different. I am asking you to use your victimhood because it's happened to you. I am begging you, for your own sake, to free yourself from the labels that isolate you from your true purpose and path in life. I understand where you are, and I am with you because I've been there, too. I didn't want to accept what had happened to me in the past as a positive learning experience, but the minute I did, I finally had a sense of peace, satisfaction, and understanding of what to do with it. It doesn't matter why or what happened to you; it matters what you do with it.

You are in complete control of your own thoughts and how you allow your thoughts to compile the blame of victimhood. I'm going to show you some indicators of how you assign *blame*. A lot of times you say, because of an event or person, "I am *stuck*". That phrase is a huge indicator that you are a victim of the effects of a situation or person. Most of the time, you are blaming that situation or person, which gives away your power and handicaps you.

I encourage everybody to sincerely ask themselves, *where do I put blame around my victimhood?* After identifying where you put blame, ask yourself, *what is my action plan to stop assigning blame?* Other questions often asked: Is it because of someone or something else that I am in this position? Where in my life am I stuck that I am allowing "my" story of what has happened to me to hold me down? What am I going to do about it? I know what my clients would do. They would take action the minute they understood that this was hindering their growth.

Now that you've answered all of those questions, you can be aware of when you are being the victim and manage your victim thoughts. The best course of action for stopping victim thoughts is to replace them with the truth, no matter how devastating the truth is.

Now that you have stood in the truth, I want you to create another truth for yourself: *Today is the day I choose to be stronger than my story and to no longer be the victim.* Own it, stand in it, talk and work through it by seeking outside resources because it can help to save you some heartache.

When you're ready, go to your safe place and decide whether you need outside help. The choice is yours. You know what is best for you. You know when it is safe and okay for you.

When possible, try simply letting go. A good way to do this is to identify what your cords are connected to. I have my clients imagine that they have a bunch of cords that connect them to everything that has ever happened to them, whether it be good or bad. I have them imagine that these cords are nasty, thick, dark wires that are stuck to them on one end and, on the other end, hooked to the story of what happened to my clients that makes them feel like a victim. The main calling of the cords is to suck the life right out of you to ensure that you never move on. The cords want you to constantly feed them negative draining energy. The other job of the cord is to keep you tethered to your story of victimhood. The cord has many jobs. Your job is to cut it off at the source.

It can be very difficult to let it go; if you can just imagine letting everything go, you see how easy it can be for you to cut the cords. Sometimes it's about stepping out of the box to get a new perspective on how those cords are connecting you to the emotions of being a victim and, more importantly, the fear of moving forward without an identity. However, those cords are connected to a victim's identity, not your true identity. The victim identity is a dark black cloud that is hiding your true identity and who you really are.

So, cut those cords and let your victim identity float away while holding on to the lessons that victimhood gave you. Just do it—cut the restraining cords so they can't hold you back anymore. Just leave them behind. There is no reason to look back at the discarded cords, since you've already received the lessons. So now you can fly with the wings those lessons gave you. Please know that I empathize with your pain, hurt, and struggles of being a victim. But I know you can be so much more, and I'm so glad to see that you're ready to fly high.

I'm going to share an inspiring client story about a victim conquering (through choice) the hardships that victimhood brings. The story features an adventurous, sweet sixty-five-year-old retired nurse who jumped out of planes to save lives. Let's call her Carol.

Carol was a victim of the effect of her son's and daughter-in-law's controlling, destructive, disrespectful, manipulative actions that drove kind Carol to live as a savior in order to be a part of her son's life. Her son's devastating decision to no longer allow Carol to see her cherished grandchildren broke her heart into pieces and caused her to be a victim of the effect of her son's decision. The minute after her son made this decision is the same minute that Carol unconsciously chose to continue to be a victim.

A little more about Carol. Carol dreamed that her retirement would be filled with her two grandsons. She wanted to be able to have fun adventures with her grandkids to make memories that would last a lifetime for those boys. Carol wanted to be with her grandbabies so much that she moved to Arizona to be with them for holidays and to be there, so they would always have someone to go to. Being as kind as Carol is, she also wanted her elderly mother, who had been living with her, to enjoy the rest of her days listening to her beloved great-grandchildren's laughter.

Carol had no clue that she was trying to save her son. But by enabling her son and doing everything for him (no matter how ridiculous the request), she allowed herself to become her son's personal doormat. She thought she was just being a good mom and helping her son. She later discovered she was enabling her son. She was allowing him to have unhealthy behavior patterns by always being at his beck and call. She did everything his way and never spoke up for what she believed was right, mostly because when she did speak up she was reprimanded by not being allowed at family events. For her, the most harmful consequence of speaking up was being told she was doing everything wrong and wasn't good enough, even though she was trying so hard. She cared so much about her family. But by doing all this for her son, because all she wanted was to be appreciated and loved, she became a victim of the effect of her own life's circumstances.

Carol woke up one morning excited to go pick of her grandbabies, completely unaware that it would be her last time. She had a normal day with the kids. They were playing outside, eating Oreos, and she was simply letting the boys be kids by allowing them to get messy and get chocolate all over their cute faces.

Sadly, Carol had the choice made for her that she could no longer see her young grandchildren, whom she adored. She became stuck in the victim mentality because she felt lost and without a purpose when she had this choice made for her. She was angered and frustrated with her son for doing this to her and her family. She didn't want to move, grow, or live without her grandkids.

She was fully trapped in the victimhood until one day her husband came home with a business card for an inspirational life coach. Let's just say she wasn't very happy with him at first, but she knew that she needed something to get away from pain of being a victim. She was sick and tired of giving all her power away. She was exactly where she needed to be to start her healing process.

The minute the two of us met, we both knew that God put me in her life to help her heal this wound. I thank God for putting us in each other's lives, because after months of coaching, she made the decision to take her power back by deciding that she would never be walked on again and that she deserves respect and kindness because she is more than good enough. In this moment, she decided not to be the victim anymore. She decided that if her son couldn't give her the respect of honoring her boundaries, she didn't want him in her life.

What a powerfully painful moment for my client Carol to be able to say, "As my son, I require more from you and I am willing to sacrifice being able to see my grandchildren to be free from the victimhood chains that were wrapped around my voice, keeping me from speaking and living because it wasn't what I had planned."

More than anything, she still can't imagine her life without them. She continues to miss them every day, and that will never go away. But now she is free, with the clarity and understanding of where her life will go now that Carol is not a victim to her son's decision any longer. He has taught her so much about standing strong and never sacrificing the truth of who she needs to be, a powerful child of God. The most incredible truth is that she will love those kids until the day she dies, and love will forever connect them. She says surrendering all of this to God has been her greatest blessing.

(Carol's story is dedicated to those two little boys who won't get to embrace the most compassionate grandma in their lives, to look up to even after all she had done for them. I would love for those boys to know that she loves you guys more than life itself and that if the choice was hers, she would be with you through thick and thin. She is the most loving, dedicated person I have ever met. I am so honored to call her my friend, to be her coach and to be able to teach her to stand

in her truth, own it and live by it. Carol, thank you for choosing to be free from your victimhood.)

15

GRIEF IS HEALING

LOSS IS MORE THAN YOU CAN SEE

Loss is generally connected to a major transition. Loss is a feeling where you know you will never get *it* back. Loss can be hard to swallow at times.

Most people see loss as a completely negative thing. However, what many forget is that, as with everything, loss is in our universe for a reason. I believe that reason is so that you see how much good you do have. It is a way to get a new perspective so that you can cherish what you have/had and what you've learned from your loss. Loss is heavy, yet you can learn and grow from it to become stronger. I believe that loss is meant to teach us to be grateful.

People lose all sorts of things. People lose people. People lose themselves. People lose material things. Some of the common losses people are affected by are the loss of a loved one, a partner, children, parents, friends, pets, dreams, and even material things such as a home, a car, or even a laptop. People lose control of their emotions. Things that cause loss are being an empty-nester, divorce, cancer, death, and health issues. The list of things we lose could go on and on.

I lost my future: I lost my future of being a cosmetologist, being a college volleyball athlete, being active, and being able to be a biological mother. I lost future relationships with my adopted brother and biological brother. In losing my relationship with my genetic mother, I lost having a mom by my side when the bad happens. I lost her being able to see me grow into the beautiful, amazing, inspirational woman I am today and having a grandma for my future adopted children (if adoption is God's plan for us). As many do, I lost the love I needed from the people missing or taken in my life. This loss is a hard loss.

What have you lost? What future do you believe you have lost and what future will you create that is healthy and courageous to replace the one you originally lost?

What most people forget about is that material things can cause a huge loss, too. Don't be quick to disregard a material loss. It is, in fact, still a loss. I know that material loss is hard to give meaning to and you don't want to admit that you get attached to materialistic things, but we all form attachments. It's a part of living and being human. I encourage you to look at those material losses and give them due credit. Allow loss to guide you to find gratitude, especially in the loss of things that are meaningful to you.

Don't forget what a loss really is and what it can look like. It means different things to different people, but don't drown yourself in your loss. All of us lose certain things in our lives and experience loss. You cannot change the fact that someone or something is no longer in your life. Uncover the hidden beauty in your loss and don't be afraid to stand in it and learn from it. Be aware of it—that will help you stay present. Use your loss and make something good out of it.

GRIEVING CAN BE YOUR WAY

Grief is beautiful and natural. There are different forms of each stage of grief. You know that grief exists. For some reason, you resist and avoid grief. Everybody experiences it on their own level and in their own time frame, and it hurts everyone differently. The typical stages of grief are denial, anger, bargaining, shock, guilt, depression, reflection, self-doubt and loneliness.

If you are grieving, the ten stages of grief are a great tool. I listed the most influential tools and added my own spin. I want you to be aware of what they are so you can use them to full advantage. If you can see that you're in one of these grieving emotions in any time of your life, then you can see that you are possibly grieving. If you know that you are grieving, then you will understand that you need to give yourself the time and space to work through it.

We all go through a specific grieving process, but some people can relate to the ten stages of grieving more than others.

Grieving is healing in the long run. The worst thing that you can to do to yourself or others when experiencing a loss is to have expectations that you or they must heal in a certain way or specific time frame.

When grieving, please allow the natural flow of grief for yourself or others to take its course in your way or theirs, no matter what the loss is.

It is easier to partner with the emotions of grief than it is to fight them and try to overpower those emotions. Don't judge your grieving or others' grieving. Just let it happen naturally because that it is how the process will work for you and not against you.

Grieving is for you. It is your tool. It is your friend. It is your helper. It is a gift. More than anything, it is the most powerful way to move on from something that is hurting you. Grief is so uniquely catered to everyone that there is not one scientific way that people grieve. You can't remove it from your life, nor can you change it. The fact is that something or someone is no longer in your life.

Grieving is a natural process. The natural way to grieve is to let your heart talk for you and don't allow your thoughts to control your grieving. Allow yourself the heart space to help you heal. Your thoughts are tricky. They will tell you how to grieve and when to grieve but keep it simple and let it be so that it can work itself out naturally.

You may forget that you grieve everyday life and the things in it. For example, a paycheck. You may grieve not having the money you thought you were going to have because you put in the hard work to earn your money. I think this kind of everyday grieving gets ignored the most, as though it's not that bad or like it's not a big deal. However, it really needs attention and space from you. Really look out for what you may be grieving and what it needs from you to heal. It's possible that you could be grieving something and not even know about it.

Grief has its own plan. Its own way. It knows and understands what you need. You need to pay attention to how you can help yourself, so you can heal. Give yourself plenty of time to relax, heal, rest, and rid yourself of distractions. Give yourself the space with nothingness. Give yourself the permission to cry, weep, and fall apart, but pay close attention to how long you stay there. Ensure that it's a healthy period of time. If you are unsure if it's a healthy amount of time, I highly recommend seeking professional help to release your grief.

I have grieved so much and for so many people in my life in such a short amount of time. I have grieved my mom, my dad, my brothers, my adoptive parents, my biological family, my step-grandparents, my grandpas, my best friend's dad (Scott), the kids I nannied, my miscarriages, my foster son, the ability to enjoy eating, and one of the hardest yet, my husband's grandma, Grandma Ehrick.

Grieving is so much easier when you find the love inside what you once had. When I lost all my previous family and friends, I grieved in a very unhealthy way. I was sabotaging my grief by trying to control it, labeling my grief, and by believing that there was something wrong, that I was doing it wrong. I wanted it to stop. It hurt so bad. I couldn't believe that the people in my life kept leaving me.

My coaching of grief changed immensely when I became the life coach of a widow. I began coaching her and her son through one of the hardest grieving processes: the passing of her beloved and the death of his father. I started to watch how much she wanted to stop the process by trying to control it and label it. She was working so hard to distract herself from the needed grieving process. Holding this family during the hardest transition in their lives gave me the gift of recognizing a pattern that I saw in them and every client I've ever coached through grief. They repeated the same pattern that I did. They worked to control and label the process and distract themselves. They weren't in the moment. They weren't taking the time and the space to deal with it then and there. They were dealing with their grief in the unhealthy way that many of us have.

After creating my grieving process of letting my heart grieve in the moment, I lost my role model, Grandma Ehrick. My sweet grandma was slowing running out of breath. This process started right when I became a coach. I instantly felt the fear of "What if I lose her?" I also felt the instinct of how I had a choice in how to walk through this grieving of eventually losing her. I chose to be present with her, upfront about everything, ask her about her fears, her doubts, and to enjoy the time we had left together. I got to hold her fragile body and inspirational spirit while she cried and, because I used my process, I was able to enjoy every minute of crying with her.

Don't get me wrong—I wanted to ignore the truth that her condition was worsening, and she was leaving me. I decided to embrace our relationship even more, which made the process so much easier. I made the worthwhile choice to see her on a weekly basis, even if I was sick and needed to pay my assistant to drive me to visit her. The best lesson that I could have possibly received from her is to be real, to be true to yourself, and to be true to God.

Grandma Ehrick helped me use my heart to grieve and to grieve in the now. She reminded me to wear my heart on my sleeve. I will be forever grateful for what she did for me before she got sick and the gifts she gave me when she was sick. She was such a vulnerable, honest, open, courageous person. She taught me to be like her. She allowed me to see the true core of the deepest, darkest truth of her pains and fears.

This was the woman who gave me so much closure from my past, by listening to me, holding me, and never judging me. The closure she gave me in the moment was the most powerful closure that can be received from grieving. This doesn't mean I didn't cry and have emotional releases because she had given me so much power and understanding. She was a great friend. She was the best companion. I could talk to her about anything. If I could have named her, I would have named her "True Unconditional Love". That's why the section on unconditional love is dedicated to her.

I know working through your emotions in the moment can sometimes be embarrassing but turn that into vulnerability. I know being vulnerable is scary, but it is worth it. Make the choice to jump into vulnerability to help you get through your grief. Vulnerability adds rawness and openness, which allows you to embrace most emotional moments. Sometimes the only time to deal with something is right there in the moment because your mind, body, and spirit know what is best for you. So, lean into your vulnerability when you can. Hold on tight and allow it to do its work. You'll love the ride because the destination is learning what your emotions and pain mean to you. The ride is also great because you get to enjoy the memories and moments with the thing or person you lost. Be present with your grieving. Enjoy the roller coaster ride.

Choose the healthy path to grieving. Choose the path where you choose a partner; allow that partner to be grief. Just let your heart do the work.

16

PRACTICE MAKES PERFECT

HOW TO BE EMOTIONALLY RESILIENT

I'm so excited to show how to be emotionally resilient. This is one of the things that I wish I would have learned at an early age. It would have helped me so much. The hard part of being emotionally resilient is that you have to work through a multitude of emotions all at once. You have to be able to grieve and work through the emotions that arise from what is going on. On top of all of that, I am asking you to be present and find the good in it while it is all happening. This is one of the ways that I achieve true success and happiness in my life.

Everyone sees their emotional pain as the worst thing that has ever happened to them. The truth about emotional pain is that it is incredibly painful. You know that is the truth. You just forget that there is the whole other side to your pain. The other side to your pain is learning how to turn our pain into emotional resiliency.

Emotional resilience is defined as adapting to the most painful and adverse times of your life to see them as an opportunity to be stronger. Emotional resilience is turning everything bad in your life into something good. It's about being resilient to your pain despite what it did to you.

However, this is an opportunity to develop resilience that serves you. It is important to develop and practice a response to your personal pain, stress, and pressure in healthy ways. Some of the best ways to practice emotional resilience when it comes to stress and pressure is by leaning into it. Use stress and pressure to guide you to learning a way not react to it. Instead, use it for healthy fuel. It's a long process to become emotionally resilient against your stress and pressure as you sit in it and learn from it. So, every time it comes up, it won't be a big deal, because you will learn from it and you will know how to sit in it. You will experience the pain anyway, so you might as well partner with it and use it for good.

Unhealthy responses can make it a hundred times worse and cause unwanted emotional patterns that become chronic and repetitive. Experience and allow yourself to lean into those horrible moments and take them as the learning experiences that they are instead of the worst thing that ever happened to you.

Obtaining emotional resilience is easier said than done because you have practiced only diving into the bad of your pain and only see it as good or better (after the fact) instead of while you are going through it. Learning from it and being present during the pain doesn't mean you are not going to react and get angry or frustrated. However, it does mean if you practice it enough times, your emotional resilience can be a tool and resource that allows you to live in a more calm, relaxing, stress-free environment.

The best way to achieve emotional resilience, clarity, and calmness is by honestly looking outside your pain in the moment that you're going through your pain and find the good in it. While you're hurting, it's your job to find the good. It's also your job to figure out what you're going to do with the pain and how it's going to make your life better. At the beginning of your learning process of how to be emotionally resilient, find one good thing to focus on each time you're hurting. I know I'm asking you to do the impossible, in the moments when all you want to do is lose yourself in the pain. You go through pain for a reason; the reason is that it is meant to teach you and make you stronger. Why not use it in the moment? It will help you develop more emotional resilience when you practice the attacks while you are in the moment and decide if you going to react. Most of the time you have no control over your initial reaction, but once you recognize it, you have the choice to do what you want with it. You do have control on how long you stay in that state of mind and dwelling on whatever happened; it has run its course, so let it go. The most important trick to becoming emotionally resilient is practicing it over and over again. This is such a powerful mindset that you should make it a daily priority.

PRACTICING YOUR RESPONSE TO STRESS

Stress is an inner feeling of pressure or tension. Stress is an accumulation of overwhelming feelings of anxiety that often causes trouble breathing. You feel as though you are suffocating. You have the feeling that you have no control. Stress takes over your whole body. Stress puts your body into panic mode by sending negative energy throughout your body. It tells your body and mind that there is no way out. Basically, stress makes you believe that the worst thing ever is happening, that you have no control, and that there is no solution. I don't have to tell you what stress is or what it feels like, because everyone has undergone stress at some point in their life.

Once you let stress get to you and you have a reaction, you're trapped in the stress. Stress is one thing on its own but add in a reaction and stress will have complete control over you. Remember you have a choice to react to your own stress or not.

The stress in your life is supposed to be stressful, but you are the one to turn your stress into good or bad, positive or negative. As humans, we are designed to handle a lot of stress. It's in our DNA (deoxyribonucleic acid) and our nature to be able to handle and balance many different things that come your way each day. Typically, weforget that it's normal and that it's just a part of life to have stress and to deal with stress. Unfortunately, you don't just leave stress as stress. You feed it energy and give it a reaction. This is where it turns into a problem. The problem is that it can become a learned behavior, where you create a habit of always reacting to your stress and creating it.

If you want relief from stress and the reaction that comes with it, here is a tool to use in the moment and on the go. The most important part of this exercise is seeing your stress escape your mind, body, and soul. If the exercises below aren't the right fit for you, I encourage you to come up with your own analogy for stress release.

Start by taking a deep breath as you imagine bringing all your stress into your hands, where it turns into a big ball of stress. (Your eyes can be open or closed during this exercise; But you should see some type of ball.) When you use this exercise, it doesn't matter what environment you're in, because you're just going to concentrate on the ball and let everything in the background disappear. Many of my clients like to imagine something like a big beach ball, the kind with the yellow, blue, white, and red stripes. Some clients create the ball in their hands and some blow it up. If you like the choice to blow up the ball, then take three breaths and imagine that each breath you put into the ball is a huge breath of stress leaving your body.

Remind yourself how good it feels to just let all your stress go into the ball. Allow it to build up and get as big as it needs to until there is nothing left to fill it with.

Now, keep your eye on the ball, concentrating on the stress escaping your mind and body and going into the ball. Once your ball is as full as it can be, and you have nothing left to give it, get ready to let go of it.

There are many ways my clients like to get rid of their stress balls. Some of my clients like to simply let go of it and watch it float away. On the other hand, other clients like to get rid of the energy around their stress. They do this by playing a game of baseball with their beach ball of stress. This game is played by pretending to swing a baseball bat and hitting the stress as hard and as far as they can out over the infield, past the outfield, and into the parking lot. They play this game until all the energy is completely gone. They like to end by winning the game; it makes them excited to move forward and meet their goals. Use whatever analogy helps you to de-stress. You get to decide to do what works for you when you are releasing your stress, as long as it's safe and right for you. As always, you are the judge of that.

PRACTICE YOUR REACTIONS

Learn how to practice becoming unresponsive to how you react when others push your buttons. Button-pushing is when you allow something or someone to push a personal button or push one of your boundaries. If someone does or says something (or if *you* do or say something) that doesn't align with you, it's like someone is profusely poking at an angry bear.

These buttons could have a value behind them or just be red-hot buttons. For instance, a lot of people's buttons would be pushed if they saw a young child not open a door for an elderly person. This is because your personal value is connected to your trigger. Your values are a gateway to button-pushing. You know that your values are the core of who you are, and you hold on to your values as the absolute truth for yourself and what you believe in. Watch out for people triggering your values and be aware of how you're pushing others' buttons.

When your buttons are pushed, you light up like an elevator with every floor clicked. Each floor you go up, you are triggered more; it uncontrollably sends you over the edge. This causes you to be super angry and frustrated. Generally, you think that you can't believe that they pushed your buttons, that they should have known better, and how dare they walk on your values? This is another type of conditioning pattern you have the choice to change. Your response is your choice.

The first step is to identify and write down what all your buttons are or at least as many as you can think of. Use that list to pick apart the buttons you want to bring awareness to and let go of.

Ask yourself these questions to uncover your buttons: What irks *you*? What is it that causes *your* buttons to be pushed? It is people, places, things, expectations, taking things personally, etc.?

The second step is asking yourself if it's worth it to have the reaction and lose yourself in it? How does taking things personally trigger your buttons? Ask yourself, *do I want to respond to the situation by having an emotional reaction?*

Third, it is smart to step back, take a couple of deep breaths and look at the big picture before you react. When others are involved, it's wise to look at the other person's side of the story and understand that your buttons are made from your unique experiences. Most likely, no one will understand them but you, even if others have gone through the same thing.

The fourth step is to not wear your buttons on your sleeve. Create a boundary where you don't allow people to push your buttons; be aware of the emotions that surround your buttons. Try to save your reactions for learning moments or when your buttons are unconsciously pushed. If you do choose to play out your reactions, learn from them. When you're ready to get back in the world and play with the way your buttons are pushed, you now have a choice to act out or set aside your reactions when a button-pusher arises.

Fifth, if you have a great support system in place that you can trust enough to practice with, I highly recommend doing so. This partner should be someone who will not take your reactions personally, who is aware to the point where they can hold that space for you to practice in, who will respect your frustrations and your values and won't react.

Recognize that you have a choice—no one can push your buttons without you.

How to Set Healthy Boundaries

I have an amazing client, Gina, who works with an array of business owners and gives a lot of her services away for free. She ended up frustrated and unsure how to set boundaries. Meanwhile, her clients have learned to expect that she will continually work for no cost. She came to me feeling trapped and needing to clean up her mess. Gina was sick and tired of where she was, and she was ready to do something about it.

The new boundary she is setting will be making clients pay for everything she does—every client and every service. The best part of her setting this boundary is that she has learned how to value herself and her business. Now that she has set this boundary, she is seeing growth, her clients are happier, and, most importantly, she is happy. Gina is fulfilled in knowing her company is finally heading in the right direction. She is sticking with her boundaries even when it gets hard because she knows that it's easier to live this way. She loves taking action with her clients and her boundaries. Setting boundaries is simplistic and so important because it creates healthy energy between you and your relationship with people and your boundaries. Don't be scared—it's worth it.

As you learned earlier of how to take your wall down, brick by brick, you have the opportunity to set boundaries to help you prosper in life. A healthy boundary is when you set a line in the sand between you and all your relationships. The best way to set a boundary is to think about why you need one, the purpose of the boundary, and if it's truly necessary to set one (though it's almost always necessary in all areas of your life). After those thoughts are established, you need to walk yourself through the game plan of how you are going to maintain the boundary and how you take action on it. Many times, you will set a boundary and there will be internal or external pressure or distractions trying to take away your boundary. It is important to make your boundaries a priority.

Making your boundaries consistent is vital. The best way to be consistent is to always follow through. The second you don't follow through, your mind and the outside forces know, and you lose faith in yourself. Most people struggle with boundaries because they don't want to hurt people. Sometimes, they don't set a boundary because the relationship is too much work, even though it makes it harder without a boundary. Others don't make it a priority, because they don't see the importance of boundaries. You may need to be so uncomfortable that it forces you to change and establish boundaries.

You can set a personal, one-sided boundary at any time. Some people don't respect your boundaries and there is nothing you can do about it except take charge of yourself by setting a boundary for yourself. You can keep your personal boundary a secret or you can tell someone else; it's whatever works best for you.

Boundaries are super unique and personalized. Do everything you can to make your boundary support your lifestyle and what you need. Set your boundary by putting the line in the sand with whomever or whatever is causing the boundary trigger. Don't allow people to cross your boundary line, no matter what. Listen to those triggers and allow them to help you build a healthy boundary. Setting a boundary is all about defining your values and rules; it is about saying what you are and aren't okay with. Your boundaries are your livelihood; they are meant to protect you and relationships. Without healthy boundaries, you are just going to be walked all over. Don't be afraid to make boundaries, say to yourself, *Do I need a boundary, yes or no?* If the answer is "yes," grab on to your courage and use it to drive you to define your boundary.

A lot of times, the desire to please other people becomes more important than the boundary and your own sanity or happiness. More importantly, you will become the passenger in your life, allowing other relationships to take the steering wheel. This can also cause you to burn out. You need to have an emotional and logical connection to it, so strong that nothing will make you change your decision to keep your boundary.

Write out your boundaries so you can be reminded of them every day. Always remind yourself of the benefit and why you're doing it in the first place. It will be hard work at times, but it is always worth it. Enjoy having healthy boundaries. Watch how your life changes and how your relationships grow.

17

JUST BREATHE

THE POWER OF BREATHING

This technique is very simple and basic, but don't underestimate its power. Did you know that breathing through your nose brings mental clarity, releases tension, detoxifies, and alleviates stress?

The best way to get centered and relaxed is by utilizing belly breathing and creating a great environment for yourself while you're breathing. Belly breathing is breathing from your diaphragm and not your chest. I know being told to breathe makes you think "I know how to do that already." (You do know how to breathe, but not with the purpose of relaxing, letting go, and being present.) You forget the power it has. Honestly, you forget to breathe all the time. You forget that if you just take a deep breath, it will get you out of your problems and take you back to reality. Most importantly, if you just breathe you can connect with yourself and you will become aware. In those moments, you are present.

Breathing can diminish anxiety or feelings of being overwhelmed. How lucky are you to have this natural breathing technique? Everyone can benefit from learning how to breathe better. Breathing is a gift from our Higher Coach. It's a tool everyone was born with and should use every day. You can use this tool to be still and present in all aspects of life. When you get into a situation that causes you to react or attack, stop, take a deep breath, re-frame, breathe again, and then make a choice. Never underestimate the power of God's breath.

BREATHE ON PURPOSE

When you are first learning to breathe, don't judge your breathing. Don't worry about if it's right or wrong. Just give it a chance. Give yourself time to learn how to breathe and have the patience to become good at using your new tool. You can use it anywhere and everywhere.

Start by finding a safe place, if available. In this space, you can sit in a chair or stand. Once you are good at it, you will know how to breathe on the go.

A lot of my clients like to close their eyes while practicing their breathing so that they can connect to their body and concentrate on their breathing. An add-on that my clients love is adding some soft, relaxing music to their space. Once your setting is prepared, you can begin the breathing technique.

There are two ways to breathe on purpose. The first one is great for day-to-day breathing and for beginners. The second is best-used when you are extremely anxious or when you are having a panic attack and can't get control of your breathing.

For daily breathing, start by inhaling through your nose, taking in all the air particles that you can for four seconds. Hold this air in your lungs for two seconds. Slowly exhale through your mouth for as long as possible. Once you're a pro at breathing, hold the air for six seconds.

If you are serious about achieving relaxation, clarity, calmness, and mental freedom, you should practice this breathing technique on a daily basis so that you create a healthy habit. Tons of amazing breathing experts recommend setting a chime for every hour as a reminder to take a breath and relax. Some of the new technological advances have made it so that watches vibrate and remind you to take a break and breathe.

The second breathing technique is for people who have lost control of their breathing. I see many clients who suffer from uncontrollable anxiety and panic attacks that make them feel exceedingly trapped. They get so overwhelmed that they forget to breathe.

Start by inhaling a deep, long breath through your nose. Hold it for three full seconds, and then blow it out as slowly as you possibly can for as long as you can. Repeat these steps no more than two or three times one after another. Be careful not to pass out.

It's definitely not for daily use. It's only for those days where you've lost control of your breathing and you need help. I can't wait for you to see how much better you feel to be free from your anxiety and panic attacks. You should practice using this type of breathing every time it happens.

I would like to thank my hypnotherapist instructor, Sherry Gilbert from Illumi Life Therapy, for teaching me this technique, allowing me to bring it into my practice, and letting me share it with you.

See where breathing is missing in your life and do your best to practice this. You will see that breathing can make a huge difference!

18

THE POWER OF HAVING AN ANCHOR

ANCHORING

Typically, when you hear the word anchor, you think of something nautical. However, I want you to forget the ships for a minute. I *anchor* my clients to one of their five senses or something spiritual on a daily basis. This is not a physical anchor that doesn't allow movement; instead, this type of anchor encourages you to center yourself mentally and helps you remember your purpose. While on the journey of finding an anchor, make sure you are safe and anchoring to something or someone safe. Ensure that your mental health is safe before choosing to find an anchor. Remember, the choice is yours.

The five senses are the best tool you can use to anchor yourself to something. For example, during a hypnotherapy session with one of my clients, I anchored Gina to a scent. The scent was something I picked especially for her, knowing she needed grounding, clarity, stability, and to breathe. She needed to find presentness in the moment. I knew that she needed something to connect her to her goal. When she was hypnotized, I taught her to stay anchored to this scent and how to find her center on her own. This is her experience and one of the best examples of anchoring. Gina explained her experience to share and teach you:

> Brittany and I were in a session and after discussing my need for boundaries from my ex-husband, she decided in the moment to hypnotize me. She had me close my eyes, get comfortable, take deep breaths from head to toe. She taught me to clear my mind, set my baggage down, and to not lose sight of my session's real agenda. She told me each time I pictured a body part of mine, my relaxation would triple with each breath I took, and it did. Then she told me to picture a park, a place that would be full of nature, a place that made me feel comfortable, where I could just be myself but also have a jungle gym for kids to play (knowing I have small children, who bring me much joy) and put all this inside of my park.
>
> She made me put wooden posts into the ground for the fence surrounding my park, and each plank of wood had a different word, which would empower me to stand strong in what I needed to fix, build or work on, to keep my fence strong and protected. Brittany shared

that during the whole session, she was waving a bottle of oil under my nose that I chose prior to our session; unknowingly to me, since my eyes were closed.

During the hypnotherapy, she asked me to visualize many of the people in my life that I would consider my angels, whether they were alive or no longer with us; these people were supposed to be with me inside of my park. My angels represent so much to me. They are my pillars of strength, and during hypnosis I was able to clearly define which angels I can lean on the most. When picturing these people, I was instructed to take deep breaths as she placed the scent beneath my nose. The fence I had built later turned into a bubble, and I now have a clear image of me and the people closest to me inside of this barrier, safe and having fun. After my fence became a bubble, I was able to let the good people in and for me to watch the unhealthy people fall on their bottoms because they couldn't get in. I watched my ex-husband bounce right off my protected bubble. It's the greatest feeling ever to have this anchor and boundaries to support me. I was instructed to both breathe the scent in but to also imagine the smell and connect myself to my deep breaths. I came out of my session feeling refreshed and relaxed, slightly emotional from working through hard feelings, but centered and calm. I had already planned a trip to San Francisco months before this session and was instructed to focus on my healing, relaxation, myself, having fun, and finding my boundaries. She asked me very specifically to set my problems to the side and focus solely on my adventure.

Once I landed in the city, I immediately headed to my Uber to meet a girlfriend for lunch, then to shop by myself afterward. Walking around Union Square, the most amazing thing happened. San Francisco Union Square trees smelled like my anchor scent! Every step I took in this beautiful city, I instinctively took a deep breath and was able to fully relax. I had no idea the power of anchoring until that moment, and it literally moved me to happy tears. I felt my boundaries finally fall into place, I felt my unhealthy patterns break apart. This may seem like a super unorthodox way to create boundaries and feel good about them, but it is the single most relaxing experience I have ever had, something that is almost indescribable until you've done it yourself. Every time I smell this scent, I am reminded to reinforce my boundaries. I even bring the bottle of oil with me to meetings with my ex-husband, so I can anchor myself.

I am so grateful that Gina allowed anchoring and boundaries into her life, because now she has a great resource to help her through the challenges in her relationships.

An anchor is an amazing tool you can attach yourself to for emotional support. It can be a positive memory, a loved one or best friend who has been a good influence, a favorite place or a safe place, etc. You can use this anchor to keep you on track with your goals or keep you from going over the edge when hurting. You can also use an anchor when you are releasing emotional baggage.

FIND YOUR OWN PERSONAL ANCHOR

Memory Anchor:

You can start with finding a positive, healthy, happy memory and bringing it alive again. The anchor you choose should have a wonderful, powerful charge to it. Imagine this with your eyes closed and your body relaxed. It may be very cool and beautiful for you, like the first time you remember running on the beach: how good the sand felt between your toes, the laughter of the families you heard while you were running, and the way the sun brought light to your face and warmth to your whole body. Find your inner anchor and don't forget that healthy memories can help you find hidden strength.

Relationship Anchor:

There are different options for this. You are able to call on a loved one who is alive or no longer with you. You can dig into the past and present to look for a loved one you trust and ask them to come and support you and mentally know that they are there. For example, during a hypnotherapy session I would ask a client if they would like to bring in a family member from their past or present life to help them walk over the finish line. This can help you celebrate big moments and wins. It can also help you stand up to someone who once hurt or abused you. There are so many amazing opportunities when you are open to anchoring yourself to a special relationship you trust. Don't forget the power and good energy this gives you. This can often give you the support, love, and encouragement you may be looking for.

Safe Place Anchor:

An anchor can be about finding a safe place. There's a chance that you've never felt safe, and if that is the case, create your first safe place now. You find a safe place by closing your eyes and allowing yourself to hear your breathing and relax for a moment and think back to all those memories of when you have felt safe. If you don't have good memories, make them in the moment. Imagine the things that could or do make you happy. Build your own safe environment. This is a place to go when you are having a panic or anxiety attack, or you just need a quick meditation place to escape to, so you can be or breathe. When you create your safe place, it can be from memories or present thoughts. It is okay to bring all the places, people, and things in the world that make you feel safe and put them in a beautiful place so if or when life hits the fan and the unexpected happens, you have somewhere to go to. A safe place anchor like this can be very beneficial when jumping into new things or letting go of things that no longer serve you. It can also be beneficial when conflict arise, and you need to center yourself quickly.

Physical Anchor:

You also have the choice to buy or use a physical anchor like a token or a picture, something you can physically hold on to. These are great in the moment because you can see or touch this anchor. Some of my clients like these because it helps remind them of what they've accomplished or where they are headed. Some of us are anchored to our wedding bands. I use mine to help remind me of where I have come from, the unconditional love that surrounds me and my commitment to God and my spouse. Physically touching your ring can bring you peace or sanity, reminding you why are in a committed relationship. Physical anchors are great when you have tons of excitement and nerves running through you body, because you have somewhere to put all that energy. Also, they give you something to hold on to remind you that you are not alone, you are alive, and your goals are real. Don't be afraid to have an unorthodox physical anchor, as long as it is healthy. Physical anchors can help you accomplish a lot of cool things; I can't wait to see how they help you.

Spiritual Anchor:

The last type of anchor being described to you in this book is connecting to and praying with your Higher Coach, be it Mother Earth, Buddha, God, the universe or whatever you believe in. This type of anchor is good when you are in dire need of support, guidance and spiritual healing. It is a lot of fun to anchor yourself to Mother Earth. The simplest way is to take off your shoes and place your feet in the sand, grass, or water. Anchor yourself to whatever you'd like to receive, be thankful and humble, and remember that everything around you in this moment is bigger than you are. I often anchor myself and my clients to God and Jesus. I imagine God placing a blanket of unconditional love around me, which is one of the most moving moments to be present in. This is the most common spiritual anchor I connect my religious and willing clients to, His love. Your spiritual anchor is a connection that you should try to use as often as possible. Don't be afraid to create this connection and use it to help you prosper through life. It's a lot easier to do this with someone or something else. This is what your spiritual side is looking for. Enjoy the connection and see where it takes you.

Now that you've learned about anchors, you should create as many healthy anchors as possible to help you execute your goals and dreams. Meaning, use the goal itself and anchor yourself to it. Start imagining how good it will feel to accomplish your goal and see yourself doing it. Use anchors as often as possible and see how they improve your life.

19

THE POWER OF ENERGY

ENERGY

If your mindset is negative, you can't have a healthy life. Growing up, I used to think that as long as I was positive, I would be safe. To be honest with you, I was unconsciously thinking that if I was positive, everything would turn out. Also, I used positivity as an excuse to not work through my pain. I unconsciously used positive energy to mask my pain, unaware of the consequences. Be careful with masking your pain with positivity; it will come back and bite you in the butt. The consequences can be unbearable, and it will take a lot of work to take off the mask of positivity. Don't worry, you can start to use your positive energy for good, as it is meant to be used.

Some people like the way it makes them feel to think to themselves, *If I just think positive, everything's going to be okay.* Although this thought process does not work for everyone and every thought, positive thinking remains a great way to achieve your goals and create healthy energy. For those thoughts that need a little more than positive thinking, start by taking action and building your faith. You have to make a choice to decide if you are going to use positive thinking, negative thinking, constructive thinking, healthy thinking, let the thought go, or none of the above. Always choose something. Don't just let your mind choose for you, because it will always choose the negative first.

All we're adding is a little more constructive thinking with a new kind of light. More simply put, that means having an open mind, always thinking for yourself, and having a great attitude with exceptional courage. It also means tapping into your spiritual side to believe you can. If you want to add a cherry on top of your thought ice cream sundae, think healthy thoughts to create positive energy around them.

You have a certain amount of energy every day. You have a choice to use this energy toward positive or negative thoughts. If you deplete your energy on the negative, you will not have any positive energy to give, and vice versa.

One of my friends taught me about the "Spoon Theory of Energy." I love to use this theory as a metaphor. It goes a little something like this: Imagine that you have 100 individual energies for that day, like you have 100 spoons to give away every day. (Every individual wakes up with 100 energies for each new day.) If you have an illness like me, you start with your 100 spoons, like everybody else, but just to wake up and put your feet on the ground in the morning takes ten spoons, whereas for a healthy individual it should take one spoon to get up. However, if the illness-free person is using a constant negative mindset, it might take just as many spoons or more to get up as it does for the sick person. If you are in a constant negative mindset, you are spoon-feeding yourself negativity for breakfast, lunch, and dinner. This teaches your body to be in a continuous survival flight-or-fight mode, which just takes away all your energy. So why not use your spoons for the good in life, to have fun, uplift yourself, be productive and successful?

In our society, it is common to fixate on everything that is hurting you, broken, not going your way, wrong, and not perfect (in your eyes), which causes us to create negative, wasteful energy. When you fixate on what you don't have, it creates a pattern in your mind that leaks into your self-talk and becomes a toxin. You will start to feed off the toxic negative energy to the point where you will need it; you may become dependent on the negativity. What this really does to you is, it makes you fixate on problems and creates a cycle of negative thinking and a need for negative energy. Always get out of your head to solve your problems. Don't continue the evil patterns that are self-destructive, such as fixating on what is wrong. Instead, fixate on what is right and what is going well in your life, because there is always something good if you look deep enough. I know this is an incredibly hard change because your mind always focuses on the negative because it's easier and you are trained to do so. Scientific studies have proved that your mind will go to the bad before the good.

To be clear, there are two types of energy—positive/ healthy and negative/unhealthy—for a reason. Know that negative energy has its place in the world and can be used in a productive way. I'm not saying there is something wrong with negative energy, because it is definitely in this universe for a reason and you need both positive and negative energy to live and to see life's true beauty. All I am saying is, don't allow it to drive your life every moment of every day. Use negative energy when it's appropriate, sit in it, then release it. Negativity can be productive energy, so long as it is temporary and used for the emotional support needed in those moments of growth in your life.

A good time to use negative energy would be if you have tried every possible positive approach first and you recognize that this particular situation is in dire need of a new solution. You see that using non-uplifting energy will shift the situation toward the outcome you need. There will be situations in life where negative energy will surprise you, bring you wisdom, create new boundaries, and have incredible outcomes. Don't be afraid of negative energy—you can't have a happy life without it. Without it, you couldn't see all the good energy in life.

After teaching my client how to use the technique of choosing between when to use positive and negative energy, she shared a story with me of when she had to use negative energy to get what she needed for her daughter. Her wonderful, sweet daughter had a very high fever. When she called the doctors hour after hour to get help with positive, kindhearted energy, she realized that she needed something new and she needed it now. She decided to use negative energy to shift the doctors' mindset to better understand that she needed help immediately. She knew what she was doing—she had control over her energy, and she used it toward a good, specific goal: to get her daughter what she needed to get better. Without insulting the doctors or being rude, she used her skill of shifting energy at the right time for the right purpose.

A lot of times, you can go overboard with negative energy because you have so much negativity build up inside you. Knowing this is a great wake-up call to only use what you need and be sure to express the leftover negative energy in other healthy ways. A few great ways to get rid of residual negative energy safely are to scream into a pillow, write a letter and burn it, go for a run, go for a safe drive just to drive and scream-sing your heart out. If you do not release the negative energy, it will manifest somewhere else. Give it the time and space it needs so that you do not end up taking it out on someone or something else.

Using negative or positive energy depletes your energy; it takes away both good and bad. No matter what you are doing, you are losing energy. Always be aware of where your energy is going. Make a conscious choice to be mindful of what your mind, body, and soul need for healing, releasing, and resolving.

Energy is everything. Always know where your energy is, always know how many spoons you have left. When you are unaware of your spoon count, that's when burnout will occur. Basically, if you watch your spoon count, you'll be more prepared and aware of when burnout can occur.

No one can have positive thinking 100 percent of the time, but when you believe and imagine, you change everything for the good. Apply this kind of thinking to everything you can. You have a set amount of energy spoons so use them wisely and productively; you get what you get, and you can't throw a fit. Do everything you can to create positive, healthy, energetic charges in your life.

ENERGY ATTRACTS LIKE ENERGY

The energy you carry to a situation is transferred. If you are happy or passionate, others will notice, and if you are sad or angry, others will observe and possibly absorb that, too. How can you recognize this power? Do everything in your power to awaken your energy and connect to those around you. Energy is so powerful when used properly. Awaken to what your energy can do for you. Don't be afraid to tap into this power. Energy is incredibly beautiful and will help you accomplish amazing things in your life. Always be awakened to what your energy looks like, what other energies look like, and how it radiates.

MONEY IS ENERGY

Let's talk about the elephant in the room, the one that makes everyone uncomfortable. Money. Money is an energy. It's all about the relationship you establish with it. Do not give money power over you but work with it as a team. Money is your partner that helps to provide you with nutrition, health, wellness, fun, and so much more. Money isn't unhealthy. Money ebbs and flows. You give money its own personality and connotation. Most of the time, the personality, the relationship, and the energy that you give money is negative and unhealthy. You give money a voice and you give that voice power over you.

Money is man-made. People forget that humans created money as a system to establish an economy for ourselves; money is a means for exchange of goods and services. What people created was something that stresses you out more than anything else. It is shocking to realize how something as trivial as money could control how you live and where you stand in your social circles. Most people have breakdowns, anxiety, and fear where money is involved; this is what you need to work on. Understanding that money controls so much of your life is the first step to changing the toxic relationship you likely have with money.

I suggest you take some time to reflect on the purpose of money. After defining the value of money, don't allow its purpose to change, and remember what money actually is. You put so much value on money that without it, you believe you have no life. In actuality, if you are willing to work hard for it and trust it, it will work in your favor and keep you on the right path. At some point, you gave money power to dictate your life; it is time to take your power back. Give money its rightful place.

You can get such a high (or low) feeling just from this one relationship in your life. It can be frightening when money is low; you may even lose faith. The best thing you can do is make a choice in the moment about how you react and the energy you bring to it. When you have an abundance of money, you want to be careful to not be wrapped up in the amount. Stay humble, be present with the relationship, recognize its energy, and respect it. No matter the status of money, stay centered, allow it to sort itself out, and work hard. Don't be lazy with money. Care about it, save it, and be smart about where you spend. You don't get to just have everything you want when you are working as a team with money. It's a give-and-take relationship. Becoming too selfish with money is the fastest way to watch it disappear. Since money does not have any emotions toward you, pay attention to your emotions with money.

If you want to discover your relationship with money, the first thing you want to do is get yourself centered in the way that it fully opens your thoughts and emotions. Grab a pen, paper, and some physical money or log into your bank account. Do whatever you can to get yourself into this energy safely.

1. Do you see money as a gift or a curse? If you see it as a curse, how are you going to shift your thought process and create a healthy relationship with it?

2. Are you excited when you get a paycheck and then devastated when you don't have any money left? If so, what's your plan to change your mindset and energy around money?

3. Do you trust money? Do you have a good relationship with money? If not, make a plan to change your answer and take action on it.

4. Do you understand that having an unhealthy relationship with money leaves constant voids in your life and that money is a constant series of highs and lows? If you do understand that, how will you change your energy with money based on the information?

5. Do you see money as a support system for your nutrition to fuel your life?

6. Do you self-sabotage your relationship with money? What action will you take to stop this behavior?

7. How will you let go of your insecurities around spending too much money on yourself or not enough money on yourself?

8. How will you let go of your guilt? A lot of times, people have a limiting belief that causes them to feel guilty about money. How will you feel good about making a transaction for yourself? Some people feel guilty spending money because they feel as though they are taking money away from their family. Guilt is a hard emotion to face because you have to know, in your gut, if it's right to spend the money on yourself. You're the only one who knows if it's the right thing to do. So, trust yourself to do the right thing and enjoy spending it, if it is right for you.

9. Is money controlling your life and how you live it? The most common answer I hear in my practice is "yes." If your answer is "yes," make a game plan to create freedom around your control. The best way to let go of control is to allow the natural flow of money to happen. Whatever you put in is what you will get out. So, put healthy energy and effort into it.

10. How does your relationship with money keep you from living your life to the fullest? Most of the time, money handcuffs you, keeping you from doing anything new or exciting because it's "too expensive." How are you

going to unlock your cuffs to enjoy money again? It's all about a conscious choice. Experience life without the restraints of the handcuffs.

11. Are you in pursuit of the almighty dollar? Are you still coming up short? If so, how do you plan on stopping the unhealthy pursuit of money in this manner? Most people believe that if they search hard for the dollar, they will be happy. Money doesn't want to be pursued like a hot piece of tail.

12. How will you start a healthy, fresh pattern to achieve financial freedom? If you are serious about setting this new pattern, you will need to create goals and stick to them. Do not let anything get in the way of your action plan. It may be hard at times, but it's so worth it. Imagine how good it will feel to no longer obsess about not having enough money.

13. What are you going to do when there is a financial emergency? Plan ahead so that when there's an emergency, you have backup funding. How lucky are you that money can support you in times of dire need? If you have not set up a savings account for emergencies, how will you start one today so that you don't put a strain on your relationship with money. I know that a lot of people live paycheck to paycheck and have careers/jobs that don't support them financially. If this is you, I encourage you to change your situation—then there are no excuses or problems to get in your way. If you do not have any money during an emergency, do your best to breathe and come up with a solution that supports

the relationship you are working on and maintains a healthy energy with money. Most importantly, if you are willing to trust the system of the ebbs and flows, you will build faith. During this stressful time, the best thing you can do for yourself is to stay focused on the solution and not the problem. Now you know that money is just energy and it doesn't have control over your life—you do. The emergency is temporary. Don't allow it to steal your progress.

14. How will you make sure your relationship with money gets the time and attention it needs?

15. How do you plan on enjoying and appreciating money? How will you have fun and create great memories? It is about balancing your needs and your wants.

My relationship with money was awful. I was terrified of it. I allowed it to have so much control over my happiness and my ability to try new things because I was so scared of being poor. The pattern I had with money was just like everyone else's. I experienced the rainbow of the highs and the frightening lows. There were definitely more lows than highs until I changed my relationship with money.

All the medical bills and becoming an adult came at the same time. I worried a great deal about being able to obtain a healthy relationship with my income and losing everything because of my bills.

Somebody very close to me told me that I was not successful because I didn't make enough money. This broke my heart because I believe that success isn't about money. Rather, my belief is that if I am helping people change their lives for the greater good, from the inside out, then what does money have to do with success? I needed this awakening when I was being coached because of my awful relationship with money. I didn't think I deserved it and I believed that only smart people could have it. I love what I do so much that I didn't want to get paid for it! This awareness taught me I had to feed myself from the fruits of my labor and provide for my family to truly be successful. One, so that I would always feel good about what I am doing and, two, so that I don't burn out. Most importantly, if I don't charge for what I do, I'm unable to see the value in myself and the life-changing services I provide. If I don't invest in myself and find worth in what I do, how am I supposed to teach my clients to invest in themselves and value their relationship with money? More than anything, I needed to figure out how to work *with* money because it was stealing my happiness and the possibilities of running a strong company where I help people be their best selves. Working alongside money has made it so that I am more present, more productive, and happier than ever. I am helping people and feeding my family. My life is so much better now that I have achieved a great relationship and energy with money.

What is your story with money and how are you going to change it? Write your story out like mine. Enjoy creating a new synergy with it and watch your stress fade away. Enjoy seeing your relationship with money bloom into one of the healthiest relationships you have.

20

CREATE HEALTHY COMMUNICATION WITHIN YOUR RELATIONSHIPS

EVERYTHING IS A RELATIONSHIP

It is important to see that you have a relationship with most everything in your life, including family, friends, money, business, exercise, health, pets, your home, and electronics. Everything is a type of relationship. I have a relationship with my husband, my backpack, my feeding tube, my family, friends, animals, my clients, and much more.

Healthy communication with everything you have a relationship with is incredibly hard to do. Most everybody communicates in a negative and draining way within their relationships. For example, you yell at your cell phone when it doesn't work fast enough or properly. You get worked up and upset and waste a ton of energy by communicating in an unhealthy way. Do everything you can to communicate in a healthy way within your relationships.

A healthy relationship is a two-way street, traveled with a partnership that fuels you in a productive way even if the relationship is complex. If you don't strive to create healthy relationships, it will create toxic relationships instead. Viewing everything in your life as some type of a relationship can help you create strong bonds and deeper understandings. It is important to find a way to develop healthy patterns and a partnership within your relationships.

I'll give you an example of a healthy relationship with money that becomes unhealthy. Let's say you have lots of money, you are happy with it, you trust it, respect it, and you're excited about creating more. However, the minute you spend it or don't have it, you treat this relationship with disrespect and a lack of trust. This is where it gets unhealthy. Instantaneously, you have started to think about what you don't have and how you will ultimately fail without it. You forget about the benefits of having a healthy relationship with your money. A healthy way to build trust in your relationship with money would be if you looked at it as a relationship and start to have the trust that money will come and that all relationships have ebbs and flows.

Take some time to look at all the relationships in your life. It is important to look at where your relationships need improvement. It would be wise for you to figure out where each relationship is draining you or how the relationship is serving you. If it's not serving you, it is draining you. If it brings you nothing but toxicity, it may be time to say good-bye to the relationship. Never totally get rid of a relationship unless you are sure that it is unhealthy. There is no storytelling and no excuses when it comes to making this decision to let go of an unhealthy relationship. There is only the pure truth that the relationship is toxic and unhealthy. Ultimately, when you say good-bye to the relationship, you give yourself freedom from the toxicity of the relationship and the relationship itself. Cutting ties may be very hard for you, especially when it is the relationships with the things or people you love, but it is more important for you to be free from the toxic and draining energy. Letting go is the best thing you can do for yourself and the relationship.

If you see that the relationship is good and serving you in a healthy and supportive way, look for more ways to acquire goodness from it and spend more time in the relationship. Give a healthy relationship the nutrients it needs to grow. When you are working on your relationships, be sure to look out for red flags, button-pushing, and set your boundaries.

COMMUNICATION IS ESSENTIAL TO RELATIONSHIPS

A huge part of any relationship is communication. Often the importance of communicating effectively gets overlooked. There are many types of communicators. One type is indirect communicators, ones who beat around the bush. I also coach people who are controlling, too direct, blunt, over-the-top, and in your face. As well, I see communicators who are bullies and overreactors. There are also communicators who stay silent, allowing room for assumptions and for people to walk all over them; in turn, silent people tend to become resentful.

A common relationship that I coach people through is one where one party is incredibly controlling. This causes huge communication issues because it is the controller's way or the highway. The submissive party is silent because the meek one is scared to start a fight or face conflict. The submissive person is fearful of how mean and dictatorial the other person can be, and the quiet person is left unheard and scared.

Find out or research what type of communicator you are. Note that I do not have all the forms of communicators listed. It is important to know what type of communicator you are to understand how to improve your relationships. If your communication style isn't listed, do yourself a huge favor and explore deeper into the other types of communicators.

One of the hardest types of relationships people have to work on is their relationships with other people. Relationship with other people are difficult because you are in your head, worried, insecure, and not present. When you are in the conversation and you are not present and not actively listening, it only takes a few seconds to react and experience a trigger. When you are communicating presently, a lot of energy is exerted to fully hear what the other person is saying, and you digest it completely, especially while they are still talking to you.

I know that a lot of people get trapped when they are trying to communicate effectively. That's okay. Never give up. You can always just restart the conversation and look for new tools to keep yourself out of the traps. There is always a solution to communicating effectively. Knowing that everything is a relationship shows you that communication is the number one way to have a solid, fun, open, humble relationship.

A few game-changers in your abilities to communicate effectively are setting aside your ego, your need to be right, and anything else getting in the way. These things are what steal your humility and prevent you from truly working things out and getting to the bottom of your issues. Once you can do this, you will bring your relationships to the next level. Some of the best ways to have a strong relationship are to be your true self, stay humble, be compassionate, and get out of your own head. Most importantly, have fun, create healthy boundaries, cry together, lean on one another, share moments together, and live your life to the fullest together. I urge you to challenge each other to be the best you.

When people miscommunicate, it can cause major problems. It is extremely important to communicate openly, honestly, and directly. It's all about what energy you bring to the conversation.

Some of the worst things to do in a conversation or in life in general are to run from your problems or to sweep issues under the rug. Remember, rejection of any kind doesn't give you an excuse to leave the relationship or the conversation. Running away is a crutch you use when you don't want to face your problems. If you find yourself running or burying the issue, understand this is why there are problems with your communication and your relationship to begin with. You must be willing to stay awake, focus on the solution, and work toward a growth-oriented, healthy relationship. When you are prepared to communicate effectively, beware because the other person may not be ready to be productive. This is not an excuse for you to react or to go back to sleep. If you want to have healthy relationships, you must be willing to put in hard work, have fun, and let the issues go; stop taking everything personally. Don't forget that this relationship is a priority for you. If it's not, you may need to look deep and reevaluate the relationship. What's the point of working on something that you can't prioritize or that you don't find important? If your relationship isn't working for you, you may have to start fresh and build a new foundation. At any point in any relationship, you can grab a new tool kit and build something better and stronger. Most of the time, that's exactly how relationships adapt and become stronger.

Every time you are about to talk to another person, make sure it is the right time and space for them and for yourself; this will make or break your communication within the relationship. The best way to communicate in a relationship is to be direct and honest. Be sure to discuss with the other person what you're looking for, what your needs are, why you're talking to them, your limitations, vulnerabilities, and fears. Vulnerability comes with no guarantees that the other person is going to hold the space in the perfect way you want it. Don't judge it and be present with the situation. You'll never get your ideal response; don't expect the reply to be exactly what you want to hear.

To be a successful communicator, you must be open, honest, and ready to listen. You have to make space to think about what the other person is feeling, thinking, and wanting from you. You have to be willing to set your own problems aside to see the other person and listen to what they are saying. This will help you stay present and in the moment. You should strive to communicate outside of the problem and lead the other person to focus on finding a solution. Refrain from giving your opinion or advice to the other person. More than anything, people just want to be heard and understood. The best communicator listens intently and can reflect in a passionate and non-robotic way.

Now is the time to get out a pen and paper to answer these questions that are meant to bring awareness to the relationships in your life and help you communicate more effectively:

1. What relationships in your life need immediate attention?
2. What actions do you need to take for those relationships to improve?
3. Is the way you communicate within your relationships healthy or unhealthy communication?
4. If it is unhealthy, what goals can you set to create healthy communication? How will you take action to improve your communication?
5. Do you communicate in a stressed-out way that drains your energy and stresses the other person out as well?
6. If anyone talks to you in a draining, stressed-out way, how do you react? Is now the time that you would like to stop this unhealthy communication style?
7. What relationships are toxic and draining your energy and which ones are worth working on?

8. How does knowing you have a relationship with everything in your life change things for you? Now that you are awakened to it, how can you impress yourself by improving all of your relationships?

I know it's asking a lot of you to see relationships in a new light, but once you create this healthy pattern of communication within your relationships, you will find that you are better understood, and you don't have to face unnecessary conflict as often. Also, you will find yourself enjoying communicating with people, bringing an overall sense of improvement to the bond and the opportunity to create good memories. Most of all, your relationships will become stronger, more reliable, and more resilient.

Don't forget the power of making strong, healthy bonds with the relationships that you have in your life, such as relationships with people you care about, chores, personal health and wellness, work, material items, and finances. Relationships are a gift to us. Every time you work on an old one or create a new one, remember that it's totally worth it. Keep in mind that you don't always have to work at your relationship when they are healthy. It is important to just be in your relationship and have fun.

21

Awakening

Wake Up—You're on Autopilot

Being on autopilot means just going through the motions, sleeping through life, and being numb. A great example of being on autopilot is when you are driving somewhere, and you don't even know how you got there. The problem with being on autopilot is that you miss out on everything, since you are just going through the motions, allowing life to just pass you by and making few to no decisions or deep connections. You are also unconsciously putting up block walls, which then causes other people to miss out on getting to know you personally.

To get yourself off autopilot, you need to first be aware that you are on autopilot. Second, you have to have the desire to jump into life and start living again, fully aware of your capabilities, surroundings, and how amazing it is to be present! Once you have decided to be present, the numbness will no longer be a shield from reality. The hard work starts by facing each painful experience you have been sweeping under the rug. The truth is that autopilot numbs you and protects you from the reality of what you're going through, have gone through, or even will go through. Autopilot gives you the ability to sit back and not have to do anything. Therefore, it's important to bring those painful experiences out from underneath the rug and give it the healing and attention it needs and deserves. Enjoy the power of being able to switch off autopilot mode and know you aren't stuck there—you are in an awakening.

If you have been on autopilot even once, it is extremely easy to slip back into the unhealthy pattern. Staying awake requires constant surveillance of yourself. Going on autopilot creates a very unhealthy energy. It may seem easier to be on autopilot in the moment, but the problems and pain are still there, piling up while it waits for you; you will have to face it sometime. Face your problems as they arise and stay aware of them, so you never go on autopilot again. Being present and aware is the best way to walk through life.

AWAKEN YOUR INNER DREAMER

You fantasize about things you cannot have, and it takes you out of the real world. If you fantasize like this and make false expectations, I would like you to see how it has affected your life. The word *fantasizing* usually carries a negative energy and leaves a foul taste in your mouth. This is because people usually relate the word *fantasizing* to thinking about other women or men.

Close your eyes, take a deep breath, and try thinking or saying the word *fantasizing*. Normally, your mind will go to unhealthy and inappropriate thoughts. You don't want to fantasize about the inappropriate or unhealthy things, because it turns into a pattern of thinking about things that aren't right for you or that don't help you take action on being a good person. Fantasizing can be harmful to you as well as others.

One example of fantasizing is when women watch romantic, sappy chick flicks and expect their significant others to be the same as the characters in the movies. Women tend to fantasize about being swept off their feet, being courted, and having a partner who is oozing romance. The problem with that is that most people's spouses or partners are working on providing and do not have tons of time or monetary resources to be super extra romantic. Most men are thinking about working, coming home to their families, "extracurricular activities," and sometimes sport and hobbies. It is very hard for them to get out of the work mind frame. However, there is no excuse for not adding romance to a relationship. The moral of the story is that it is not fair to fantasize about romance, because it creates unhealthy energy and expectations. Create a pattern to stop fantasizing now. Go through all your old patterns of how you used to fantasize, choose to let them go, take action, and stop them now and forever.

Protect yourself and dream instead! Because dreaming is with hope. You can see all levels of a picture of what you could and should have. Embrace the beauty of what you really want and allow yourself to see that you can have anything and everything—you are limitless! Dreaming is beautiful and healthy. Fantasizing is not.

I have shared my dream with you, so you know what one looks like. My dream of having a purpose and being able to make a difference in how people live. My dream is to give people the gift of freedom from their mind games and emotional pain. I connected with my Higher Coach to achieve my dreams. I have made vision boards and posters, written letters to myself, and colored to find and achieve my dream. Another thing I did to triumph was asking others for help and support. I held myself accountable to my goals, and so did they. If I never chose to dream, I would still be very lost and alone in my pain and hurt. You can choose to dream, too.

Dreams are wonderful and so important. Dream today and every day. You can make your dreams come true with hard work, dedication, action, humility, and courage. To meet your dreams, you have to be able to shift them and not control them. Allow the outcome to change and go with the flow. Don't forget to have fun, enjoy the journey to achievement and, celebrate when your dreams come true.

AWAKENING

An awakening takes place in your mind. An awakening is where you are fully conscious and have you an "aha" moment that gives you the missing pieces and possible answers to your problems. It feels so relieving and refreshing to wake up, even if it's a bit uncomfortable. Awakening is that feeling that you have when suddenly you are aware of something new. Some people say I'm having a rude awakening with *x*, *y* or *z*. I think that rude awakenings are always a gift because you gain more knowledge.

Awakenings are amazing and powerful things that happen in your life. It is beautiful and healthy. I hope you have had moments of awakening in your life. If you haven't, my wish for you is that you will work hard to find them.

There are moments of awakening when you are awakened to a reality where you gain a clarity of something you didn't really want to find out. Awakening is something I really want you to pay attention to. Whether it be that you are waking up to your partner's infidelity, or waking up to your dream job, it is still very important. Look for the moments in your life when you were on autopilot and you were awakened. Use them to help you recognize when it is happening again, so you will have the opportunity to be awakened. These moments are healthy and important for your growth. I know that sometimes this can be painful, but it's worth it.

LOVING YOURSELF

You have realized what true love is. You also know that you should not be a pleaser. Now you need to learn how to put yourself first.

People usually say that putting yourself first is selfish. When you love someone, you make them your priority, you think about their needs, desires, and interests. You stop caring for yourself.

Yes, you should give importance to those you love, but why does that mean you should stop caring for yourself? In fact, you should make loving yourself a priority. Why? If you can't care for yourself, you can't be there for others, nor can you teach others to love themselves or to be leaders. If any of this is running in your mind, continue reading to discover your answer.

Those who you love also love you, and want to see you happy and healthy. When you sleep well, eat healthy, and exercise regularly, you feel so good. When you are overworked, feel a lack of energy, and irritated, this not only affects you but also affects your relationships. No one would want to see you that way, especially not your loved ones.

When you are overworked, you cannot enjoy life, you are stressed, and you are anxious. Everything might feel like a chore. Do yourself and your loved ones a favor: awaken fully to loving yourself and never forget the value it has. Take the time to recharge and rest. Fill up on love so that you can be a leader in loving yourself.

How to Prevent Burnout

There are only twenty-four hours in a day. How many times do you find yourself wishing for just a few more hours? A lot of my clients constantly say to me, "I just need more time." The truth is, everybody feels this way. There will always be things to do; there will never be enough time to do everything you want to do in one day. With hard work, planning, and dedication, you will have more time to do the things you need to do. In turn, you will have more time to do the things you want to do.

Managing your time and creating priorities is important, but so is resting. Once you find a balance between resting and doing the things you have to do, you will find that you have so much more time. Learning to delegate and prioritize will help increase your time and ability to rest.

If you struggle with delegating and prioritizing, you must find a way to accomplish these goals because it will drain your time, productivity, and balance if you don't. It will also cause incredibly painful burnout patterns. These types of burnout patterns sometimes put you into a stress mindset that causes anxiety. Most importantly, this causes you to be in fight, flight, or freeze mode. This is why resting, and delegating is so important to your health and your sanity.

The best way to delegate and prioritize for rest is to simply plan out your day to the best of your ability (either every morning or every evening). This is so you can have a checklist of what needs to be done and how much time you have to get it done. It also provides organization, simplicity, and a sense of being prepared.

Things may come up suddenly or there may be an emergency. When that occurs, you will put the emergency first and re-prioritize later. It's important to remember that instead of cutting out your rest time, you need to reorganize your schedule and move to-do's to different days. I know that everything has a deadline. I understand the pressure. However, I also know that burnout is so much more pressing. Burnout causes you to make mistakes. Your emotions get the best of you, and you lose your focus and centeredness. Therefore, you must make rest your priority. I get it—you're an Energizer bunny (just like me), but that doesn't mean you don't have to take out the batteries every day to let them cool off and recharge. Sometimes to recharge you need a vacation. A trip can help you to relax and rest and give you a place to revamp.

Rest is one of the most powerful things you can do for your mind, body, and soul. If you desire true balance and success, give yourself rest as often as needed! There is no shame in resting. You are not lazy. If your inner critic is causing you to feel discomfort, you know what to do: put your inner critic to rest. Don't be afraid to take time for yourself and rest. You will find true balance and you will be free from your burnout. When you are well-rested and free from burnout, the possibilities are endless.

THE POWER OF TAKING A COMPLIMENT

As women and men, everyone dreams and talks about wanting affirmation from those in their lives. A great question that I get asked from the men I coach is "How can I be expected to continuously compliment her when all she does is reject me and the compliments I give her?" I think every woman and man have had similar conversations in their relationships that involve that question. The story usually goes just like this: a significant other walk into the room, sees their partner and tells them how beautiful they are, or how much they want them. Sadly, the other shuts them down immediately (which is unhealthy) by asking, "Why? I look like a fat cow today!" By using those draining words, you are shutting down any energy or movement inside the relationship, possibly ruining future opportunities, and hurting the complimenter. The truth is, everybody has heard someone shut down a compliment before. You should work on accepting compliments without shutting them down. Heck, after a while, you may even start believing the compliments to be truth! Create a pattern now that you believe the compliments—that's the first step to taking a compliment. Always remember, it's a choice to take a compliment. Compliments are verbal gifts, so be open to receiving them.

You may be uncomfortable taking compliments, as you tend to believe they're not true. You may have a story or a limiting belief that supports the decision to deny words of affirmation others are giving you. You may even argue or brush it off. You may take the compliment lightly, without considering the other person's intentions or feelings. When you lack the ability to take a compliment from others, it can discredit the other person. They may even question giving future compliments. Why would you want to create a situation where you can't accept a perfectly good compliment from someone who sees something great in you?

Though there are many reasons people don't accept compliments, there are a few big ones that stand out. Sometimes it's because people are afraid it would make them seem egotistical or self-absorbed. Others may feel awkward or uncomfortable and be unsure how to respond.

Accepting a compliment is taking it to heart and trusting that the other person means well. Dig deep and figure out why you cannot take a compliment. It is important for you and your growth to be able to accept a sincere compliment. It is super important to have a desire to learn how to take a compliment. It matters as much for you as it does for the other person. If you can't learn to take a compliment for yourself, then accept it for the sake of the person giving the compliment. This doesn't mean to stop learning to take the compliment for yourself. This just means that you have to work even harder, but it is well worth it. Accepting a compliment to the point where you truly believe it helps build self-belief and self-worth.

If you are building confidence (or doing any of the work in this book), it is imperative to take a compliment, truly accept it, and believe in yourself. People will notice and be so excited to watch you finally take a compliment instead of being rejected for being kind. For you to be able to take this to heart, you will have to make a choice right now to sincerely thank other people for compliments even if they sound outlandish or crazy to you. This is the easiest way to create a pattern to accept compliments. Start by taking the compliment on the surface and then learn to accept the compliment on a deeper, internal level. Not every compliment you get will make sense but see how fun and good it feels to accept and give compliments. My favorite compliment to give is to the people who are smiling for no reason. I love to tell people that their smile brightens my day and thank them for sharing their happiness.

YOU ARE NOT ALONE

The most common things humans share is our pain and suffering, whether it's the same or not; humans are all hurting and suffering in one way or another. Humans have a lot more in common with each other than anybody cares to believe. You think it's better to go through life alone, pretending that no one else has or could be hurt like you. The truth is there are probably hundreds of people who have lived through the same type of hurt as you have. I understand that this is hard to believe, but when you start to believe that you are not alone and that you share commonalities with others, it gives you humility and strength to work through it alone or with others.

Everybody wants the world to be a better place! It's funny how it is hard for you to recognize what you have in common with other people. As a society, we have been through way more common pain than you give credit or would like to admit. Everybody has pain, has suffered, and has been neglected or abused in some way or another, big or small. You forget that everybody is in this together and that everybody has felt that pain, yet you tell yourself that you are completely isolated and there is no one else like you. This just is not so! The best way to make the world a better place is to recognize that everybody is hurting, reacting, and trying to survive. If you can see that pain, it will help the world to be a better place because you will be more patient, kind, and understanding and less reactive. You will also see the beauty in the world, even through all the suffering. You will also see the gorgeousness of the world by simply seeing the pain that is meant to be out there. Always remember that the world could not be beautiful if you didn't have the opposite to compare it with. You can't see the good without knowing of the bad.

There is so much more to the world than your pain and hurt. There is a world full of people who want someone else to connect with over their pain. You just have to look for those people. Please know that you are not the only one hurting. You weren't intended to be alone, and there are too many people and resources to support you in your times of need to not take advantage. The best thing to do when you are hurting and alone is to know that you are not alone and that someone else is going through this and understands, just maybe not through your exact lense. Wake up to the fact that humans have so much in common with each other; this will make your healing so much easier.

Your Purpose Is Calling You—Listen

Keep an open mind because your passion could come to you at any age and at any time, when you least expect it. Embrace all the wonderful things that come your way, as long as they make a difference in your life and in the world in a good and healthy way.

Throughout your lives, you are told that if you find your calling and purpose you will be completed and fulfilled. The truth is that your calling and purpose can and will fulfill you. It is imperative to work through your baggage, because your pain can cloud or even ruin the process of receiving your purpose.

I think a lot of people wish they were born knowing what they want to do and who they are. It would be awesome to wake up and know those things already. Some people are born with the knowledge of what their gifts and callings are, and they are able to tap into them right way. Other people unconsciously block them and don't know how to tap into them at all. Some hear a voice telling them that nursing, journalism, economics, or volunteering is the right fit for them—that could be your Higher Coach or intuition calling you to your purpose. Others don't feel anything and have to work really hard to find their purpose—this could be for many different reasons.

For some people, there are lots of trials and error that must be worked through before they find their true purpose. I find this to be the fun part, having the opportunity to try on your purpose. On the flip side, my clients find this process to be very draining and frustrating. They honestly hate this part because they just want their purpose to be laid out in front of them—they do not want to do the work to get there. Do your best to enjoy the journey of trying on purposes. It will lay the foundation for your true and ultimate purpose. Don't be afraid to try new things until you get to your true purpose. Every purpose is worth something and it is not a waste of time. I have tried on many purposes that got me to where I am today. Do your best not to label, control, or push this process because that will create stress, pressure, and anxiety. Allow the process to happen naturally. It will be so much more enjoyable for you. Hold on to the faith that you will find your purpose.

A good indicator of whether you have found your passion is the emotion surrounding your purpose. If the emotions are enjoyable, satisfying, and uplifting, that's a good sign because it signifies that you're following your calling or purpose. When you feel those emotions, listen to your purpose calling you. If there are no emotions around it, there are other ways of finding your purpose and knowing it is right for you.

Most people learn their calling in the most difficult of circumstances. Hard times are often the moments when clarity strikes, and you are able to find your calling. How lucky are we, the people who have had hurt and pain in our lives, to have the pain and suffering turn into something good that makes us happy? The more pain and suffering you go through, the more that you have two options to pick from. You can use your pain and turn it into purpose or you can allow your pain to take you into the depths of the oceans and drown you in darkness. Why wouldn't you want to turn the bad into purpose? I encourage you to use these lessons to find your purpose. Be brave enough to believe that you're meant to live a life full of magic and miracles.

TURNING YOUR PAIN INTO PURPOSE

Everything happens for a reason; all of your pain exists for a reason. It is all about how you see it, what you do with it, and how you allow it to drive you through your life. Every experience in your life is a step toward your destiny, but you are often too blinded by the pain to see that everything has a purpose. If you change your perspective toward painful circumstances, it will eventually be easier for you to take each challenge as an opportunity for growth. It is especially difficult to accept there is a positive reason for loss or grief. During times of pain, people rarely see the blessings in the experience. Loss helps you discover your inner strength, express love, and appreciate life so much more.

Life is a metamorphosis where everything is designed to mold you to be your best, whether it is painful or not. Take a caterpillar for example. It goes through several changes before, during and after times of chaos and pain. The caterpillar sheds its cocoon and emerges with lovely wings. These wings allow the butterfly to soar to great heights. More importantly, it allows the butterfly to have freedom from the pain of being a caterpillar and the hurt of growing into its true self. You should take time to take deep breaths, absorb, step back, and really understand what your experience means to you.

Turmoil and chaos may seem like a coincidence, but often, you create this chaos and turn it into stress and displeasure. Therefore, it is your job to realize that everything works together for a purpose. People around you might view events as normal, but for you, the events have a real and deeper meaning to you. Remember that your pain is your pain. No one can tell you how you should feel. I have had times when I let people make less of my pain because I didn't realize that it was meant for me and me only.

Pain, whether physical or emotional, makes us feel neglected and somewhat worthless. Instead of wallowing in sadness over your pain, use the following tips to turn it into purpose and do everything you can to never feel worthless or neglected again. You have the power to turn your pain into something bigger and better. Why not do that instead of wallow?

Remember, look in the present, not the past or the future. Letting go of your past allows you to feel more at ease about your future, and it gives you the opportunity to be in the present. You will understand that what you thought were failures are often indicators of great success. Never label something as a failure, because you never know what it is going to turn into in the future; just look at me. Don't be afraid to turn your failures into true success. When you look at everything as learning opportunities, success is just around the corner. You will see more successes in your past, present, and future. Leaving the past and future where they belong and staying in the present moment is by no means easy. You must work hard at it;

otherwise, you will never reach your destiny of turning your pain into purpose.

When you crowd your mind with thoughts about the past or future, you leave no room for the beautiful present moments that could help you in the process of turning your pain into purpose. A great way to clear your mind is with daily meditation, prayer, or doing something relaxing to allow yourself to find a space to clear your mind of everything that is crowding it with distractions. Just let your pain in so that you can work through it and maybe understand its reason for being. This daily ritual gives you the opportunity to get the peace of mind and rest you need for your mind, body, and soul. You yourself are asking for a recharge and replenishment, consciously or unconsciously. Do this daily meditation so that you can give your mind a rest while your mind is changing. Turning your pain into purpose is amazing, hard, and exhausting work.

Everybody needs to find somewhere or someone to surrender their pain to. Surrendering your pain is a great relief. Some great ways to surrender your pain are grounding it, writing it on paper and burning it, and declaring something healthy in its name. Use this to fuel you. For me it is easiest to surrender my pain to my Higher Coaches: God, his son, Jesus, and the Holy Spirit. The problems of our past will become the bridge toward great opportunities in our present. Do your best to surrender to your pain to whatever higher power you believe in. Learn to listen, reflect, and turn your pain into purpose.

22

FINDING OPPORTUNITY

A GUIDE TO A WIN-WIN OPPORTUNITY

A win-win situation is an event where all parties involved are equally satisfied with the results. The win-win agreement cannot just be about looking at what is in it for you but about taking the other person into account as well. You will learn to look at a situation from an angle where the results will benefit all parties involved. The win-win agreement always helps improve your interpersonal skills as you relate with people on a day-to-day basis, because you have learned to look at things not just from your perspective but from theirs, too.

How can you achieve this agreement in your relationships with others? Below are several elements that are key to the win-

win agreement in all areas of your life. You can use these same tools to create a win-win situation with yourself.

1. **Desired results** – These are the results you want to achieve by the end of the process. Aside from a detailed description of the kind of results you want, this also includes a date by which these results should manifest. For example, you want to start having a weekly date night with your significant other; you guys don't always agree on the date-night activity. Your desired results would be to have a nice, fun, enjoyable time with them to strengthen your relationship, so the activity is almost insignificant. Knowing this will save you from any sort of frustration around doing what they like to do or what you prefer to do. If you both decide the result is to enjoy time together, make that your true objective. What results do you desire?

2. **Guidelines** – These refer to the parameters that are put in place that will help you achieve your results. Guidelines are comparable to the rules and boundaries of the win-win game. Guidelines are typically forgotten, but rules are very important because without rules, there are no boundaries. What are the guidelines orboundaries necessary for you to obtain a win-win situation?

3. **Resources** – These include budget, people, and other amenitiesthatwillbeusedtohelpyouachievethedesiredresults. For instance, for your product launch you will need a marketing team, a technical team, a finance team, transportation, etc. For a date night, you will need a budget and possibly a babysitter. What resource do you need in order to have a win-win?

4. Accountability – This refers to the specific time given for the results to manifest. Accountability may be the most important component of a win-win situation. To be accountable means you do what you say you are going to do. This allows people to trust and lean on you. It allows yourself and others to know that you are going to take action. I know that tons of people struggle with being accountable, but now is your time to make a change. Being accountable is the way to go; it will increase respect and dependability in all win-win situations. This time frame enables everyone to work toward a specific goal. Furthermore, the overall goal can be broken down into smaller goals. It will be beneficial to all parties to know the progress they are making. It will also help all parties to know whether they are on the right track toward achieving the desired results by a specific date. How will you be more accountable and what do you need to do to achieve this goal?

5. Outcome – Outcomes can be equally good or bad. These are the results of the win-win decisions you made. Do your best not to fixate on the outcome but on enjoying the journey of getting there. Sometimes the outcome is a compromise more than exactly what you wanted or how you wanted it. If you choose to meet in the middle, do it with true selflessness and excitement for a win-win. The outcome is fun because it can change, or it can turn out how you planned it. Sometimes it can be the opposite and it can give you something you didn't even know you needed. What outcome do you want from the win-win process?

6. **Execute** – This is where you do what you say you are going to do, and nothing can get in your way. You are committed and ready to execute the plan you have created! Have fun when you execute. Enjoy the process of executing all your hard work. What is your plan of execution and how will you take action on it?

7. **Celebration** – You celebrate the outcome, good or bad, embracing the moment. First with yourself, then, with those who were involved in the win-win, celebrate with them, and then with a trusted loved one who has supported you throughout your journey. Sometimes all it takes is just a conversation with someone else where you share the gratitude you have for following through with the win-win decision. How will you celebrate and who will you celebrate with?

SEE OPPORTUNITIES EVERYWHERE AROUND YOU

Did you know that you live in a world that is bursting with opportunities everywhere? If you opened your mind to them, you would be presented with options that could lead to success. Don't let these opportunities continue to pass you by. Below are several ways in which you can learn to spot different opportunities around you.

It is important to surround yourself with creative people. Do you have that one creative friend who seems to see the world in a different way than you do? Did you know that creative people's minds are tuned to see things from a different perspective? Thus, they are quick at spotting opportunities. Spend more time with such friends, and if you don't have any, make an effort to find some. Thankfully, with numerous social media sites, meeting new people has never been easier. After hanging around them for some time, you will realize that their creativity as well as their ability to see opportunities is beginning to rub off on you. It is natural for you to take on their different ways of thinking and inspire and influence you toward your new perspective. This works well when you appreciate their company and hang around them as often as you can. Surround yourself with people who see the world differently so that you can see yourself and the world more creatively.

How to awaken to facing your problems? Where there is a problem, there is an opportunity waiting as a solution. Write down pain-points that are a source of constant problems for you. Purchase a little notebook that should be specifically for jotting down problems you want to find opportunities in. In your free time, take out your notebook and brainstorm on possible solutions to these problems. If you don't have the free time, make the time! Think from the perspective of how you would like a certain problem to be solved. Would the solution be of value to you? Chances are, the same solution may prove to be invaluable for others as well.

Changing your mindset is a key component in seeing opportunities that you need to seize. Do you find yourself rejecting unorthodox ideas? Learn to think and see things from a different perspective. Do not be quick to write off something simply because it is different from the way you view things. Allowing your mind to think of "out-of-the-box" ideas will help you spot opportunities more often. Enjoy the process of changing your mindset and allow your mind to play with the unorthodox options. Have fun with it. Take in the new fun and creative ideas. You have no idea where they will take you.

HOW TO CREATE SOMETHING OUT OF NOTHING

Is your mind full of great ideas that you would love to see come to life, but you cannot seem to find the right way to do this? Do you want your ideas to forever remain just that: ideas? You've probably heard stories of people who became so successful and yet started with very humble beginnings. They were able to make something out of nothing. If you were to examine their lives closely, you'd find that they had four key things in common. These things form the pillars of the ability to create something out of nothing.

The first pillar of commonality is creativity. You cannot expect to find your greatness by just recycling someone else's ideas. If you find someone else's ideas to be wonderful, you must add your own twist and your own perspective so that it turns into your idea, because it comes from your unique experiences of pain and joy. You need to create or find your own niche. So how can you do this in a world where discoveries are being made every day? In order to learn to be creative, you need to believe that you are. Once this happens, your mind will open to opportunities and ideas that you may have overlooked before. You will learn to observe what is going on around you because you are already living in a world that is being run by the greatest innovators. You could simply live your life the way everyone else does. Of course, it's easier that way, but in doing so, you stop thinking of how you can make your life different and better. I encourage you to look at the world around you and form new connections by identifying your needs and coming up with solutions for those needs.

When you want to create something out of nothing, look for things that are nonfunctional or broken that would be fun or exciting for you to creatively change or look for something that you don't need to completely change but that you can improve and update. When you find this answer, you may feel a sense of fulfillment, happiness, and joy. You may feel that you have to do this to provide safety for yourself and the people around you. You may feel that you have to do this because it's your destiny. Whatever emotions you feel, let them fuel you to make a difference.

Everybody has a chance and the opportunity to create something good for the world. You just have to be willing to tap into it. The best way to tap into it is to believe that it's there. You have so much undiscovered and unused potential. You have creativity stored inside of you, but it takes creativity to find your creativity. Put your mind to the challenge of using your untapped creativity. You and I know that you have so much more to offer the world. Don't be afraid to tap into those undiscovered parts of your life. It may take some patience, guidance and trust in yourself to help you get you there.

The second pillar is resources. Resources are important for executing a goal, especially when trying to turn nothing into something. You will need to look at whether you have the right resources to turn your idea into a solid solution. You may have to come up with new ones. Start by making a list. The best way to come up with new resources is to dig deep into the resources you already have and figure out how they work into your plan of creation. Use the resources you already have to jump-start your idea. If you don't have any resources, you have the opportunity to find and create new ones. All your untapped resources are waiting for you. You can always find the resources if you are willing to look hard enough. It's all about how badly you want to create something out of nothing. Sometimes you need to create resources out of nothing in order to create something out of nothing. Take that challenge as a tool to drive you to create a resource that hasn't been created yet. I double-dog dare you to meet your true potential to create something out of nothing.

Value is the third pillar of commonality among people who turn nothing into something. Value is the need for the potential you will be creating, as well as what it means to you and if it's worthy of your investment. It's important to measure the value of your idea against how difficultit will be to solve it. Will it fit the needs of only a small group of people or will it be applicable to thousands across the globe? Or will it just help you and the people in your world? What you want to show the world is all up to you. What is the need for this idea in the world? If you can see value in it, you might as well have fun playing with this energy to discover the value in your idea. .

What meaning does it hold for you to create something out of nothing? What values do you have that will help you decide to dedicate your time and effort to creating something out of nothing? What values do you need to create to help you accomplish this goal? What values do you need to hold on to to make sure the process doesn't shift who you are and what you believe in? What values are important to you in this endeavor? Last but not least, what new values do you need to create for this new process and what new patterns are created in doing so? One more time, when you are creating something new, make sure your values are aligned with the person you want to be in the world and the outcome you wish to receive.

The final pillar is humility. Humility is an important pillar that people who create something out of nothing tap into. I believe that you must be humble to create something out of nothing. I think you are so blessed with the energy that comes with being humble. How can you be humble when creating something out of nothing? How can you free yourself from your ego and your inner critic when you are in a state of creation? Again, the simple answer is by being humble and present. Humility is what will help you beat your inner critic. Honestly, that is the best way to create something out of nothing. Tap into your humility and put yourself in other people's shoes so that you can see the problems that need to be addressed. Don't ever be afraid to sit in humility. Humility will give you some of the most amazing answers and ideas. I believe that the most successful people on this planet are humble, driven, and kind. I also believe that because they have these qualities, they have achieved true, long-term success. I wish that all the leaders of this world were humble. The sad truth is that people find success without these qualities. However, I believe that those people who are lacking in humility will eventually lose everything. Do everything you can to create a pattern to be humbler and see what it does for your life and the people around you. I would be willing to bet that you will have a great chance of being successful. When you can create this pattern, it will spread into your whole life, especially your ability to create something out of nothing. Enjoy your life of living in humility and appreciate the path of being humble and kind. Always lead your life humbly—you'll never be happier.

Creating something out of nothing is one of the most beautiful, courageous, fun processes you will have the opportunity to be a part of. So, tap into it and see how it feels. There's no harm in trying to create something out of nothing. When you are creating something out of nothing, it can be something small or something huge. It's really all up to you. Don't measure the results of what you create; instead, measure the joy of the process that it took to get there. Allow that to fuel you to continue enjoying the process of creating something out of nothing. Be ready for the roller coaster of emotions that come with creating something out of nothing. Stay present to your goals anddesires. Stop at nothing to take action. Do the world a favor: take your worthy ideas and run with them. Don't be selfish in keeping your ideas to yourself. You never know what impact your ideas will have on the world.

23

LAUGH MORE

ACCEPTING SMILES AND LAUGHTER INTO YOUR LIFE

Did you know that there are several choices you can make that can help you live a happier and more enriched life? Every single day of our lives, we make choices, and each of these choices has the ability to negatively or positively impact our well-being. Below are simple, yet effective techniques that will help you achieve living a happier, healthier life.

Smiling takes fewer muscles than frowning. Also, smiling releases endorphins, which are basically happy hormones. You can do so right now. Crack a smile. See how good you feel? Even when you are angry, if someone smiles at you, your lips move, too. You would be surprised at how infectious smiling is.

Once you start smiling, you will be elated to see the newfound cheerfulness around you. Remember that feeling you get when a child smiles at you, the pure joy that you can see in their innocence and playfulness? This is the exact energy exchange I am talking about.

People always want a red pill or a blue pill to fix them. They forget that they don't need a pill—they just need a smile. I want to share an experience that I have had and that I believe is fairly common among the human population. When someone is crying, hurting, or highly emotional, someone else wants to relieve that pain for them and snap them out of the problem. A great example of this from my personal life is when I was emotionally charged and my amazing husband, Taylor, smiled at me in hopes of showing me that it was okay and that the problem wasn't as bad as I thought it was. He tried to get me to breathe and calm down, so I could be present. I instantly bit off his head, attacking him, saying, "How dare you try to make light of my pain and suffering?" I used to think he did this because he didn't want to deal with my emotions, but the truth of the matter is that he was trying to do an incredible favor for me. To this day, he will still do this for me. If someone tries to lighten the mood, you should crack a smile, take a breath, and be in the moment. Take that moment to decide if you should go back deep into the emotions of hurt and pain or if you should stay in the newfound lightness.

Laughter equals good medicine and healing. How lucky are we to have the ability to laugh? We are so fortunate to be able to simply smile and know that healthy energy was exchanged.

Let someone crack a joke for you. Openly accept joy and laughter. Wherever I am—the gas station, the grocery store, the doctor's office—I always try to smile at whomever looks my way. Smiles are contagious, even when someone is being a grump. My smile is a gift from God and I use it more than anything else because it takes next to no effort. Your smile is a gift the world needs. Please use it.

HOW TO BUILD FUN INTO YOUR GOALS AND SITUATIONS

Having fun and laughing is an incredibly important part of your life; it is an amazing way to stay present. You can get so trapped in your seriousness and setting goals that you become obsessed with finding a solution or finding the perfect outcome. I know that it's hard to think about adding laughter to serious situations, but it's worth it. Truth is, you can get too wrapped up in the dullness of it all, which might make you forget to find beauty, fun, and laughter. This can cause more stress or cause you to lose sight of your goals. Do everything you can to add light and fun to every goal you make. This will change the situations and the outcome in a big way. Allow it to and do anything you can to add this in your life. Enjoy this process of setting goals with fun, high-energetic energy. The best way to start doing this is to add in one funny or humor-oriented thing to your life goals for thirty days. Then make it sixty, and then allow this energy to flow through all the goals you set. Add in as much laughter as you can. Never give up on bringing brightness into your everyday life and goals. This will help keep you from getting crushed under the weight of life's heaviness.

Allow yourself to think about how to get your imagination excited about change, growth, or overcoming a situation. I want you to imagine what the excitement will feel like as you experience it and when you achieve it. Allow yourself to put all the fun that you can into this goal and into everything you do because when you can find the fun in something, it can bring out a side of yourself, as well as a side of the goal, that you may have never seen before. It can also help you strive to achieve a goal even though it could be boring or painful.

It just makes situations and goals easier when you add fun into it. Don't forget how amazing fun can be when you need it. A lot of times, the reason why you don't achieve certain goals could be because your attitude is not allowing you to enjoy the process to the fullest. So, remember that when you are making a goal, if it's not fun and exciting, why would you want to do it? It is so important to recognize the power of fun and excitement. I'm not saying you can add joy to everything in life, but when you lighten it up, it can be easier, and I suggest you do so as often as possible. I challenge you to add laughter and joy to everything in life. We do so much better when we decide to find the good in our goals and situations, not just the bad.

You can also find humor in those situations that are so serious. Try to bring laughter and uplifting energy to those situations and make it lighthearted. A great way to look at goals and situations is to ask yourself what gets you excited, what floats your boat, and what really motivates you.

Some great questions to ask yourself when you are trying to bring laughter into your goals:

- Is your mind getting overly stressed by being too serious?
- What do you have in your life that helps you find brightness and light?
- What in your life is incredibly funny and fun?
- What fun hobbies in your life help you maintain your sanity?
- What is your humor like? How do you use it?
- Do you understand what your humor can bring you?
- Do you know what makes you laugh the most?
- Are you overthinking and need breaks? Why not add fun into them?
- How do you laugh when things aren't going your way?
- How can you bring more fun into your relationships?
- How can you laugh more at yourself?
- How can you laugh more to help fuel you through everyday life?

Use the answers to these questions to help you self-discover and set amazing, fun goals. Do everything you can to belly-laugh on a daily basis, even just for five to ten seconds. Bring as much faith, love, and hope into your goals as you can. Start by discovering what the power of laughter means to you and how it makes you feel great. Find a show that makes you laugh a lot. See a comedy live or online, go to a movie—we have so many resources. You can go online and look up just about anything to make you laugh. There are no excuses when it comes to adding laughter into your goals. Don't forget that laughter and brightness relieve conflict and tension. We all need to have fun in our lives. We all need to play all out, and more than anything, we need to laugh as often as possible.

24

BE DEDICATED TO GRATITUDE

HOW TO BE GRATEFUL

Before you can get into living your lives with gratitude, you need to address what is often in your way: complaining. You know you do it. You have moments when you automatically complain without even knowing it. You get used to complaining being the way we talk about our problems to others and to ourselves. Complaining is a pattern. We all know it's not good for us, but we do it anyway. We all complain because it's easier and safer to give away anger and frustration than it is to be vulnerable enough to talk about the truth and face our problems. We all know it's a big distraction from the happiness of life.

I'm not saying that complaining is always unhealthy. However, the type of complaining I'm talking about is unhealthy and can keep you from finding one of your most precious gifts: gratitude.

Complaining feeds an unhealthy cycle of negative draining energy. Generally speaking, complainers tend to get into the unhealthy cycle by continuing to spread a story, making the energy grow bigger and bigger, trapping them in the cycle. This cycle also keeps you from growing and finding solutions. You get stuck in the moment of complaining, which steals your presentness. Sometimes when you complain to another party, they will feed off the unhealthy energy by feeding it more, supporting it, overinvesting in it (making it their own problem), or enabling it. Once you start complaining about one thing, it will leak into every area of your life. Honestly, it's all about how you complain, what you are complaining about, and how you feed off it.

Of course, there is the healthy form of complaining that helps you talk out a problem. This type of complaining allows you to get the energy out in a healthy and productive way, remove the weight from your chest in a safe and supporting environment, and work out a solution to take action on. Healthy complaining allows you to have a release because sometimes all it takes is an honest, nurturing listening ear. When it comes to complaining, you have to be very careful because it is so easy to get sucked into the unhealthy form of complaining. You really have to be emotionally mature, present, and awake to complaining in a healthy way.

I wish that for once I could read that our mind went to the good first, but again it loves the lack mind frame more, especially with complaining. If all we think about and talk about is what we lack, then all we have is complaints. No one wants to live their whole life complaining about it. Everybody wants to live a life free from complaining, but they never do anything about it. Well, here is your chance to start on your path to becoming free from this pattern of complaining.

It starts with a choice to be ready and starting the process of freeing yourself from the pain and the cycle of complaining. Now is your chance! Take a moment and make a space where you can really think this through. Take the time you need to see how much it means to you and how it shows up for you to live free from complaints. Get to the bottom of your complaining and make a plan to get out of the pattern. Enjoy the process if you can. I did, and my clients did, too.

Here are some questions and steps to help you unshackle yourself from the vicious cycle of complaining. How often does complaining distract you from creating or enjoying your gratitude? How many times a day do you complain? Play a game with yourself and see how many minutes and hours you can go without complaining. Once you've got the minutes and hours down, start turning them into days, weeks, months, and years free from unhealthy complaining.

How many times did you catch yourself complaining while you were playing the game? What did you learn about your complaining? What do you complain about and why? Now is your chance to create a solution to stop complaining. Sometimes you learn it's not worth complaining, which helps you realize it's useless and meaningless. How has complaining affected your relationships? I'm sure that you see how much wasted time and energy you put into it. You may have noticed that the more you complain, the less people want to listen to you talk. You no longer want to give your time and energy away to something that causes you to lose sight of what really matters, which is being thankful for what you have.

This can be hard to do, but each time you complain, you need to start over and try again. Being aware of what you're doing is the first step. Congratulations on seeing your own patterns and knowing what is holding you back from gratitude and true happiness. Congratulations on seeing your complaining for what it is, unhealthy and draining. Begin teaching your mind that complaining isn't serving you or getting you anywhere in life. Thankfully, once you start this new healthy habit, the old pattern starts to lose its rhythm and will eventually give up. You will triumph because you're stronger than the cycle and you're no longer giving it any energy. For this to happen, you can't give in to the temptation of complaining, not even for a minute. Don't let it back in. It's not worth it! Instead, let your gratitude guide you and heal you.

When was the last time you took a deep breath and were grateful for the oxygen that filled your lungs? How often do you give thanks to your Higher Coach for all that has been given to you? When was the last time you looked at yourself in the mirror and were grateful that you were alive? How often have you felt gratitude for how unique and special you truly are? When was the last time you were grateful for your natural gifts and talents? When was the last time you were grateful for the opportunity to turn your life into purpose? When was the last time you were grateful for your freedom and your ability to choose? Add to this list of questions and ask yourself when was the last time you were grateful? Go through every person, every item, your pain, your suffering, and everything that makes you whole in your life and take that moment to be grateful. Make an action plan of how you will keep gratitude always in your heart.

Sometimes you need to take pleasure in being grateful for the small things in life. You will find that happiness comes to you easily when you are grateful. You can share your gratitude by telling someone what you appreciate about them and telling them "thank you" for the specific things that they have done for you. You can show your gratitude by simply telling someone how grateful you are that they are in your life. When you do, slow down, see the person for who they are, and be sincere. It is sure to make you smile with gratitude, too.

I encourage you to share your gratitude with others. Sharing gratitude with others is a very beautiful and precious exchange between people. Also, the other person may really need to hear what you have to say, and maybe they have been waiting to hear it for a long time. Maybe you have been waiting to share your gratitude for a long while, too.

If possible, have others share what they are grateful for, too. This creates healthier energy and helps you to see something in your life that you didn't see before. Maybe some of the things on the other person's list should be on your list, too. Don't be afraid to get good ideas from other people, if it feels right for you. A lot of families go around the table and say what they are grateful for. There is a reason so many families do that; it is so important to sit in your gratitude and share it.

How often do you express your appreciation to yourself and others? Do you show it as often as you think? If not, now is the time to step up and use your voice to share your gratitude. If you don't say it when you're feeling it, you can miss out on opportunities in life and in relationships.

I know that there are some people reading this book who feel as though they have nothing to be grateful for. I believe that you can always find at least one thing to be grateful for, even when life is ugly and painful. Being grateful takes courage and humility. The question is, are you courageous enough to find gratitude in the darkest corners of your life?

In addition to being grateful, you can give back to the less fortunate. You don't have to have millions in your bank account to give. Simply buying a meal for a homeless person will not only leave you feeling good but also remind you that even the little you perceive yourself to have is more than what someone else has. When you give to others, it reminds you what you have to be grateful for. I dare you to dig deep and be brave enough to share gratitude, live gratefully, and give to others graciously.

Now you're ready to write out all the things you're grateful for. This is great because you can look back at it and add to it as time goes on. You should add to it as often as possible. On your list, write out as much as you possibly can about the people and things you are thankful for. What new habits do you need to create to obtain more gratitude? What lifestyle changes need to happen for you to live in this new light of thankfulness? What kind of support do you need to obtain more gratitude? Have you ever felt gratitude before? Do you know what you're working toward? What goals do you need to set right now? What stories do you need to stop telling for you to stop complaining and be grateful? Also write out how amazing it would and can feel to live life being thankful. If you can, think of all those times when you had more success because you walked the talk in gratitude and write them down, too. Gratitude equals success.

Being thankful is so good for your mind, body, and soul. Don't ever forget the power of being grateful. I hope you can add to your gratitude list by digging deep and finding those things you took for granted. Once you find them, I would love for you to stop taking things and people for granted and instead start being grateful for them.

First ask yourself these questions to better understand the cycle of taking people, your lifestyle, or things for granted. I would like you to ask yourself: Why was I taking them/it for granted? Am I doing this unconsciously or consciously? If you would like to have more gratitude, this is the right place and the right time to find it and live by it. Everybody walks around saying, "Be positive, think positive," while I think you should be saying, "Be grateful, be grateful." When you are grateful, you bring healthy, happy energy into the world.

Here's the start of my gratitude list. Hopefully my example will give you a great starting point for your list.

- I am grateful for God and Jesus Christ and the unconditional love and freedom they give me.

- I am grateful for my great supporter, my amazing soul mate, Taylor, and the wonderful gift he shares with me, his loving family.
- I am thankful for my adoptive family and the cousin who brings laughter into my life.
- I am grateful for my aunt, my stepfather, my biological mother, and everybody who has touched my life in a positive or negative manner.
- I am thankful for my feeding tube and how it allows me to thrive and not just survive.
- I am grateful for everything that has happened to me because it got me to where I am today.
- I am grateful for my friends who have become my family. (You know who you are.)
- I am thankful for my gifts and talents. I love helping people and I am grateful for how it makes a difference in the world.
- I am grateful for all the pain and suffering that is in the world that gives us a life worth living. I know that may be difficult for some people to understand, but please don't judge my gratitude list. I know that if people don't have pain, they can never learn the true beauty of gratitude or true presentness.

This list is my deepest personal list of things that mean the most to me. Your list can be deeper or lighter than mine. All that matters is that you find at least one thing to be grateful for. Have fun finding your gratitude. Always be grateful. Living in gratitude gives you the best outlook on life. Dedicate yourself to a life that is led by gratitude. In return, you will be a leader in gratitude. (I'll let you in on a little secret: the world need lots of leaders in gratitude.) The emotional beauty and peace that come from gratitude are indescribably priceless.

25

Unconditional Love Has Hidden Beauty

Unconditional Love

Life is all about giving and receiving love. I think everybody in life is searching for unconditional love and that is why you play out so many of your emotional reactions and stories. I believe that everybody is born with unconditional love to give that is eventually stripped from you in one way or another. There are few people in this world who are blessed with knowing and having this type of love their whole life. These are people like my mother-in-law. These people generally walk the talk and share their love unconditionally. They are great examples to live by. This is why Taylor's mom is a true leader of unconditional love in my life. Because you were born with the power of unconditional love, you have the ability to tap back into it at any time. However, people have a hard time coming back home because they have suffered deep wounds, rejection, and baggage. Don't fret—you can find your way home with the light of unconditional love. You just have to be willing to follow the light and trust the journey.

Unconditional love is really what you were meant to have and share here on Earth. What you want the most in this life is to be loved and share your love. Unconditional love is when someone absolutely loves you from the inside out, is free from judging you, and loves you no matter what happens. This love is priceless. There are no requirements for having it. This love is Christ-centered. When you are in a relationship with someone who has this type of love, you feel comfortable and safe. In my opinion, unconditional love is exactly what Jesus Christ and God stand for and give to each of us.

Unconditional love is a way to try to live your life. The more you step into unconditional love, the more you can lead with love and light. You can share the beauty of what love was meant to do and be in this world. You may not realize it, or you might forget the power of love. It is way more than a word on paper or something you say to someone. It is a deep connection. It's where you love others no matter what, without any expectations.

Unconditional love is an emotion you feel in your mind, body and soul. This type of emotion fills you up with confidence, peace, and the feeling of being safe. Unconditional love gives you an emotional charge that allows you to feel whole in yourself, in your relationships, and simply life in general. Unconditional love gives you the feeling that there is nothing better on Earth to receive. Unconditional love is like a hug that lets you know that everything is going to be alright.

If you are willing to surrender and trust unconditional love, you will be able to receive and give the ultimate gift of feeling unconditional love. This feeling is difficult to put into words, because it is such an intimate connection with yourself, your Higher Coach, and people you're in a relationship with. It is almost impossible to explain this feeling without having experienced it for yourself. You'll just have to try it and find out.

My Grandma Ehrick, my husband's grandma who became my grandma, was a great example and role model of living and leading her life in unconditional love. She unconditionally gave away love to her family, friends, and strangers. Not only did she love everyone, but she taught her children to lead their lives in light and love, too. Taylor's dad, her son, is a great example of how she keeps the love alive and passed it on to him. When she loved, she loved without judgment. Without blinking, she gave her unconditional love to my drug-addicted mother, who was living in a halfway house and who had just got out of prison. Without judgment, my Grandma invited her into her home with open arms.

I met my Grandma when I was fifteen years old, and it was hard for me to understand or trust her, since I had never before received love in that capacity. Loving me unconditionally in her heart was so natural and she gave it away so easily. I always wondered if she knew how powerful that love was for me and everybody else around her.

There is never a "catch" with unconditional love, and she just swept me up and immersed me in it. This woman saw the worst sides of me, but she also saw the most beautiful sides of me. This is what unconditional love can do in all relationships. However, in order to give unconditional love, you must first take the time to give yourself all the unconditional love you have to give. Once you master that, you get to share it. It allows you to be free from walls and boundaries when either of you needs something. No matter the age or time, you completely know that the other person supports you 100 percent, has your back, and loves you no matter what—no if's, and's or but's about it!

Unconditional love does not judge. You have the ability to support the other person even when it may be difficult for you. That difficulty gets washed away by this kind of love, as it has absolute power. My grandmother treated me like a golden star, and I know she made all of her family feel this way. Being a leader with unconditional love is such a beautiful path to be on. I am so grateful that she and her family gave me the gift of giving and receiving unconditional love and leading my life with the light of love.

If you want to feel a strong, healthy emotional charge with unconditional love, you can start by asking yourself these questions. As you begin this process, ask yourself if you're open to giving and receiving unconditional love. Are you ready to trust the process and try something new? Begin by looking deep inside and wonder where and how can you be a leader of unconditional love. What are the areas in your life where you judge others, where you can instead place a beautiful lining of unconditional love? Where can you give more unconditional love? Where and how have you been seeking unconditional love? It is important to ask yourself, *Am I seeking that love in a healthy or unhealthy way?* Ask your Higher Coach to fill you up with that feeling of unconditional love and ask for your Higher Coach to give you enough to share. Meditate on that particular thing, person, object, or whatever it is you pray to, to fill you up with the beauty and livelihood of this kind of love. When you think that your life is over, and the material world is stabbing you in the back, you may think you have nothing left. However, know that no matter how hard life gets, unconditional love is still inside you. It is your *choice* to allow certain life circumstances to deplete all of your unconditional love or to be filled with so much love that it doesn't matter what life throws at you. It's all about how you want to obtain it and keep it in your life. Because I was missing it most of my life, I now will do anything and everything to continue to work on of having unconditional love in my life.

You must realize that you have the power to choose to be in any situation in your life and know that the unconditional love that you feel for yourself, your family, your friends, and your Higher Coach is more powerful than any fear-based thought on Earth. To have and give unconditional love naturally gives you purpose in this world. You can't buy it. You can't fake it. It's something you must create inside yourself and share. It is easy to obtain once you let go of all your baggage. You now have room for the unconditional love to move in and make a permanent home! Allow that to happen for your benefit. I have made an oath to myself that I will live my life with unconditional love.

I hope you can walk the talk with me and lead your life with unconditional love and never look back.

26

FIND YOUR INNER FAITH

HAVE FAITH IN YOURSELF AND YOUR HIGHER POWER

Having faith means so many things; it is to believe, to trust, and to know. It is up to you to be ready to jump in and have faith in yourself. It feels great to know that you can do anything. However, for so many, this is a hard concept to grasp, let alone live by. To live in faith is to ignite that part of yourself that believes you are going to accomplish the things that you feel are not accomplishable. Your faith comes from inside yourself. You have to believe in who you are at your core. You will have so much faith in yourself because of the guidance you receive from your Higher Coach.

You have to be willing to dive in 100 percent and know it's possible because you know you are capable of so much. Having faith in yourself is one of the most important things you can do to attain confidence. Are you ready to jump in and have faith in yourself? Now is the time.

Building your faith and confidence turns on a part of yourself that has been turned off for so long. When you turn it on, you allow it to turn into a little seed that will grow into a big beautiful flower of faith inside yourself. Having faith is such a beautiful thing. When you obtain faith, you build a trust within yourself that helps you develop a relationship with your gut instincts. Listening and trusting your gut is a huge part of having faith in yourself, which allows you to have faith in others. Having faith in yourself, being strong, and believing you are on the right path makes you so powerful. The other aspect of faith is believing in something besides yourself. Believing in a Higher Coach helps to instill faith in yourself. The more faith you have, the more abundance you will receive.

As with love, you have to start with yourself in order to share it. To have faith in yourself is the first step. The second step is to acknowledge and confirm whatever belief system you have and use it to support and guide you in a healthy way. This allows you to have a more faith-filled life. I do not necessarily care about what belief system or religion you believe in, but I do care about your having faith in something outside of yourself. I would like you to have faith in a higher power. Having faith in something like your Higher Coach instills in you the notion that you are not alone in this journey that people call life. Faith is a magical thing that will change your life for the better.

Faith is about more than you; it is about something bigger and more powerful, and it is there to help you. You can have faith that there is someone else walking beside you. They can come in any form, shape, or size you believe in. Your Higher Coach is your partner that is guiding you to believe in yourself so that you can do anything and everything you want to in this life. If you're not sure who or what your Higher Coach is, that's okay. If you don't know what to have faith in or what faith even looks like or feels like, that's okay, too. Now is your chance to find your faith and your Higher Coach!

I strongly urge you to figure out who or what is your Higher Power so that you know the lifeline you are grasping on to. Who is going to be there for you when you hit rock bottom or when you lose faith in yourself? Don't be afraid to reach out for that lifeline, no matter what it is, as long as it's supportive and healthy. If you already have a connection with your Higher Coach, how can you make it stronger?

A good way to find or strengthen your faith is to write out who or what you believe in or what you would like to have faith in. Write out the things you want to have faith in and the things you already have faith in. Write an action plan for how you will gain your faith and the things you will need to overcome to do so. Explain how your faith serves you, guides you, and supports you in all of your endeavors. If your faith has never given you this, now is the time to write out what you want out of your faith. Also, if your faith isn't as strong as you would like it to be, now is your opportunity to write out how you want it to be supportive to you and what you will do to get there. Also write down the times when you want to lean on your faith and use it. Allow this list to reflect everything you would like to obtain regarding your faith. Use this list to guide you and remind you every day how important your faith really is.

Here is a personal example of my faith. I am telling what I believe in—in hopes of helping you to find and define your own faith and beliefs. I truly want you to find your faith. I want you to do everything you can to find you faith; do not give up till you find it.

As for me and my beliefs, I am a Christian woman. I believe in Jesus Christ and all of His guidance. I believe in His unconditional love and I am beyond grateful for it. I believe that I am His daughter. I know that I am never alone. I have faith in my relationships and I trust the people around me. I have faith that people are good. I believe that everything will work out for the ultimate good. I also believe that everything happens for a reason and I don't have to know the reason. I believe that it is God's job to know. I believe in all of the beautifulness of Him. I am proud to be doing God's work in my everyday coaching. More than anything, I am so grateful to have Him to hold on to when everything is falling apart and when everything is gorgeous and beautiful. I thank God and Jesus for giving me the opportunity to have faith in myself and for allowing me to live a life in complete faith and have a life worth living. I have faith that all pain and suffering have a purpose and is a learning opportunity. My faith is believing that I was put on this Earth to do more than just focus on myself, to do more than just get by. I am here to thrive and obtain more in this world. I remember sitting with my birth mother in a halfway house during a meeting and hearing the Reinhold Niebuhr Serenity Prayer, which goes, "God grant me the serenity to accept the things I cannot change; courage to change the things I can; and wisdom to know the difference."

Thinking back, I can remember the faith, power, and strength that the Serenity Prayer gave me. I hope you can use this prayer for yourself, too. I know this prayer has a stigma but let go of that and enjoy the words for what they are

At some point, we have all lost faith in ourselves. But if you do not have faith in something bigger and stronger than yourself, you are left to wonder what happens when you lose yourself in the hurricane that people call life. What happens when you lose yourself in this world that has so much pain? The sad truth is that without your faith, you do not have that lifeline to grab on to. To have faith in yourself and in your Higher Power is so important because it gives you the ability to stand tall in a world where you feel like you are being beaten down. Having faith in yourself or something bigger gives you a purpose to live, it gives you passion, and it gives you confidence in yourself.

Whatever your faith, I strongly urge you to dive in and dig deep to emerge in something you can believe in, hold on to, and have faith in forever. This faith system is meant to support you for as long as you live. It is supposed to be there through the good, the bad, the uncertain, and the uncomfortable times in your lives. This inner faith that you have in yourself is meant to be there for you no matter what. Your Higher Coach knows who you are internally and allows you to hold on to the goodness that is inside you.

If you are struggling with believing in your goodness, your faith allows you to lean into that doubt and change it. Always remember that you are good; you came from good. You will have a healthy, vibrant life where you can breathe and live in the present moment if you just have faith in yourself and your Higher Coach. Have faith and never give up on it, because it is one of the things that are consistent and free to have in your life.

UNWAVERING FAITH

You should give yourself the choice every day of how you're going to handle life. Faith does not have any requirements besides trust and belief. It takes lots of faith to believe that your past and pain are part of a master plan for your life. However, this is the most fundamental teaching you could ever learn. It helps you to know that with the faith in yourself and your Higher Power, you will indeed be able to handle your problems, no matter how bad they are. When those moments come, and you feel as if you are at the tipping point, remember that there is a plan for you. Your needs will be met accordingly, whether it is by your own beliefs or the belief that God is watching over you and will provide, protect, and guide you to live in your true power.

Unfortunately, it is common for people to scoff at your faith. However, with unwavering strength, you will succeed! In faith, we believe in God or a higher power; we learn to trust in our Higher Coach through all our life experiences and trials.

Lack of faith can lead you to allow negative energy and thoughts; it destroys your faith in yourself or your higher power.

You need to have an unshakable confidence in your beliefs so that your faith does not waver, even when you are mocked or challenged.

Without faith, it would be impossible to view setbacks as opportunities for great comebacks. Faith drives you in the direction of your destiny so that you can see clearly that there is a reason for everything and you can use your problems as incentives to be a better you. Your faith is your beliefs—don't let anyone tell you anything different. Don't be afraid to stick to your guns and lead your life with unwavering faith. Evil and draining, dark energy will fight your faith in every way imaginable, but if you never waver, your Higher Coach will give you the strength and faith to get through whatever obstacles come your way. Be a leader to yourself and to everybody else. Always have unwavering faith in yourself. Make a choice every day to be bold, to be brave, and to use these tools to guide you to a beautiful life.

ABOUT THE AUTHOR

Brittany Ehrick is a certified inspirational Life Coach, hypnotherapist, speaker, author and entrepreneur whose leadership and wealth of expertise transforms lives. Brittany is a passionate, vibrant and motivational force whose unwavering compassion motivates others to create their true path and achieve maximum potential.

As a dynamic speaker and author, Brittany shares her extraordinary life story, riddled with struggles of learning disabilities, life-threatening health hurdles and staggering hardships, to ignite a fire of growth in others. In a quest to free herself from the destructive patterns of her childhood, Brittany discovered her purpose to bring out the best in others. She accomplished what seemed impossible and, with a guiding hand, helps others do the same.

To learn more about Brittany's keynote presentations, workshops, this book or personal appearances, please contact:

Bringing Out the Best in You!, LLC

brittanye@bringoutu.com

www.bringoutu.com